DEMOCRACY AND THE SOUL OF AMERICA

WALKING WITH GOD:
THE SERMON SERIES OF HOWARD THURMAN

DEMOCRACY AND THE SOUL OF AMERICA

Howard Thurman

Edited by
Peter Eisenstadt and Walter Earl Fluker

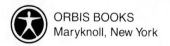
ORBIS BOOKS
Maryknoll, New York

ORBIS BOOKS
Maryknoll, New York 10545

Founded in 1970, Orbis Books endeavors to publish works that enlighten the mind, nourish the spirit, and challenge the conscience. The publishing arm of the Maryknoll Fathers and Brothers, Orbis seeks to explore the global dimensions of the Christian faith and mission, to invite dialogue with diverse cultures and religious traditions, and to serve the cause of reconciliation and peace. The books published reflect the views of their authors and do not represent the official position of the Maryknoll Society. To learn more about Maryknoll and Orbis Books, please visit our website at www.orbisbooks.com

Texts by Howard Thurman copyright © 2022 by Anton H. Wong for the Thurman Family.
Introduction and commentary copyright © 2022 by Peter Eisenstadt and Walter Earl Fluker
Published by Orbis Books, Box 302, Maryknoll, NY 10545-0302.

Library of Congress Cataloging-in-Publication Data

Names: Thurman, Howard, 1900-1981, author. | Eisenstadt, Peter R., 1954- editor. | Fluker, Walter E., 1951- editor.
Title: Democracy and the soul of America / Howard Thurman ; edited by Peter Eisenstadt and Walter Earl Fluker.
Description: Maryknoll, NY : Orbis, [2022] | Series: Walking with God ; 3 | Includes bibliographical references and index. | Summary: "Sermons on democracy and the spirit of America by Howard Thurman"— Provided by publisher.
Identifiers: LCCN 2022019680 (print) | LCCN 2022019681 (ebook) | ISBN 9781626984981 (print) | ISBN 9781608339600 (ebook)
Subjects: LCSH: Christianity and politics—United States—Sermons. | Democracy—Religious aspects—Christianity—Sermons. | Loyalty—Religious aspects—Christianity—Sermons. | Liberty—Religious aspects—Christianity—Sermons. | United States—Religion—Sermons.
Classification: LCC BR516 .T575 2022 (print) | LCC BR516 (ebook) | DDC 322/.10973—dc23/eng/20220725
LC record available at https://lccn.loc.gov/2022019680
LC ebook record available at https://lccn.loc.gov/2022019681

Contents

Acknowledgments and Editorial Note

The editors thank Dr. Silvia P. Glick for her assistance and Robert Ellsberg of Orbis Books for his support of this project. A special thanks is extended to Anton Wong and Suzanne Chiarenza, grandchildren and trustees of the Howard Thurman Estate, for their permission to pursue this publication. Finally, the editors would like to acknowledge their gratitude to Dr. Edwin David Aponte and the Louisville Institute for making possible research time from 2016–2017 for Walter Earl Fluker through the Louisville Foundation Sabbatical Grant.

Most of the texts in this volume are taken from transcriptions of audiotapes; the transcriptions were made under the auspices of the Howard Thurman Education Trust in the 1970s. When possible, we have checked the accuracy of the transcriptions against the original audio tapes. The editors have tried to retain the informal, improvisatory quality of the sermons, while eliminating double starts, some interjections and tangents, and have silently corrected obvious mistakes, punctuation, and resolvable confusions in the transcriptions. The original audio sources differ in their comprehensiveness; some include initial meditations and opening illustrative quotations, while others do not. Whenever possible, the editors have included the full sermon or lecture. Thurman used gendered language to refer to persons or people in general throughout his career, and the editors have not altered his language. The editorial procedures used in preparing this volume closely follow the editorial statement in Walter Earl Fluker, ed., *The Papers of Howard Washington Thurman: The Wider Ministry, Vol. 5* (Columbia: University of South Carolina Press, 2019), lvii–lxi.

Abbreviations

HT   Howard Thurman

HTC   Howard Thurman Collection, Howard Gotlieb Archival Center, Boston University

PHWT   Walter Earl Fluker, ed., *The Papers of Howard Washington Thurman,* volumes 1–5 (Columbia: University of South Carolina Press, 2009–19).

WHAH Howard Thurman, *With Head and Heart: The Autobiography of Howard Thurman* (New York: Harcourt Brace Jovanovich, 1979).

Introduction

Life, Liberty, and Loyalty

Coming Alive to Democracy

It has become, undoubtedly, Howard Thurman's best-known quotation, beloved by life coaches and authors of self-help books. "Don't ask yourself what the world needs. Ask yourself what makes you come alive, and go do that, because what the world needs is people who have come alive."[1] You can find it on greeting cards, in advertisements for upscale lines of clothing or housewares, or as a glossy motivational thought of the day, often with a backdrop of a rugged mountain or an inviting seascape, or with men and women jumping for joy with their arms outstretched. It has many admirers, along with a few detractors who have written to explain "Why I Hate That Howard Thurman Quote."[2] We do not hate it, exactly, but, if taken in isolation from the body of Thurman's thought and work, it can be quite misleading. Putting aside its somewhat shaky provenance— its only source is a conversation that the Catholic scholar, Gil Baillie, remembered having with Thurman as a graduate student seeking advice on what needed to be done in the world. Thurman's response might be good personal advice, implying that you should not let others set your life course, but it poorly represents his views on how one should respond to the needs of the world. Far more typical are statements such as the fol-

---

1. Gil Baillie, *Violence Unveiled: Humanity at the Crossroads* (New York: Crossroads Publishing, 1995), xv. Thurman no doubt said something similar to Baillie, who was of course under no obligation to remember Thurman's words with stenographic accuracy.

2. See Erin McGaughan, "Why I Hate That Howard Thurman Quote" (January 27, 2017), https://erinmcgaughandotcom.wordpress.com/2017/01/27/why-i-hate-that-howard-thurman-quote.

lowing from his 1939 lecture series, "Mysticism and Social Change." The mystic, he states, "is forced to deal with social relations . . . because in his effort to achieve the good he finds he must be responsive to human need by which he is surrounded, particularly the kind of human need to which the sufferers are victims of circumstances over which, as individuals, they have no control, circumstances that are not responsive to the exercise of an individual will."[3]

Thurman was always critical of self-absorption. "You can't pursue happiness on a private race track," he said in 1951, for its consequence would not be "a simple thing like unhappiness, but you get disintegration of soul." (This he argued was at the root of capitalism and imperialism.)[4] A decade later, in 1961, he argued that far too many Americans were focused on the "private fulfillment of [their] lives" to the exclusion of the "responsibility which we have to get acquainted with the facts of the world," including its less attractive aspects, such as the nuclear arms race.[5] From the time of his study of mysticism with Rufus Jones in the late 1920s Thurman was concerned with what he called the "thin line" between "a sense of Presence in your spirit" and "being a little off," unable to connect to external realities with the urgency they demand.[6] Although he was heartened by the revival of meditation and spirituality in the 1970s he also worried that a too fervent practice of the "mysticism of the life within" could lead to an unbalanced inwardness and could lead to shirking of responsibility for one's society and its problems.[7] In general, it was Thurman's firm belief that "men are made great by great responsibilities," and without them they "lack a sense of responsibility for the common life" and their internal morale and sense of identity can shrivel.[8]

3. HT, "Mysticism and Social Change," in *PHWT*, 2: 215.

4. HT, "The Declaration of Independence IV: The Pursuit of Happiness," current volume, 72.

5. HT, "Community of Fear" (Marsh Chapel Sermon, May 7, 1961), HTC.

6. HT, *The Way of the Mystics*, ed. Peter Eisenstadt and Walter Earl Fluker (Maryknoll, NY: Orbis Books, 2021), 146.

7. HT, "Mysticism and Social Action," in *Lawrence Lectures on Religion & Society, 1977–1978* (Berkeley, CA: First Unitarian Church of Berkeley, 1978), 18. In this account and elsewhere Thurman argued that the Roman Empire declined because civic religion was replaced by mystery religions that valued interiority above all other virtues, and there was a similar decay of civic awareness in contemporary America.

8. HT, "The Quest for Stability" (April 1949), in *PHWT*, 3: 311.

In the end, perhaps, there is no real contradiction between the two perspectives on personal and spiritual commitment. Perhaps what Thurman was saying to Baillie was that if you start by asking the world what it needs, you will never find your answer. To know others, first know thyself.[9] This is not an invitation to selfishness, but instead a pathway to finding your deeper connections to the people who sustain you, and to the web of interlocking communities that constitutes humanity. When you find what makes you come alive, you become the channel "through which the knowledge, the courageousness, the power, the endurance needful to meet the infinite needs of the world must flow."[10] Thurman gave this process many names: "detachment," "relaxation," "centering down," and "affirmation mysticism." It is also at the heart of Thurman's vision of democracy, as articulated in the sermons and lectures published in the current volume.[11]

This volume collects some of Thurman's most important unpublished sermons on the nature of democracy in general and democracy in America in particular. His view of democracy certainly included what is normally considered to be politics and the political, but it was never centered there.

9. This is a familiar theme in Thurman. In 1961, writing of Abraham Lincoln, he described how Lincoln's introspection and reflection on the deepest questions of democracy led to his resolution to end slavery in the United States: "Every individual has a private responsibility to discover the ground of his private peace. The core that defines for him the place where he stands in existence and its meaning, and to hold this inviolate as he seeks to discover the things in his world that can feed this. This is our responsibility." See his sermon, "The Green Bough," February 12, 1961. More generally, as he told his listeners in 1972 in "Black Pentecost: Footprints of the Divine," printed in the current volume, "the thing to remember is that the only life you have is your life, and if you do not live your life, following the grain in your wood, being true to the secret which is your secret, then you must stretch yourself out of shape in order to hear the Word and this means, you see, that you cannot come to yourself in the Word."

10. HT, "Kingdom of God" (June 1938), in *PHWT*, 2: 170.

11. If Thurman had a favorite quotation, it was surely the words of the American socialist leader Eugene V. Debs to the judge who in 1918 sentenced him to prison for opposing World War I. Expressing a passionate identification with the needs of those on the margins of society, Debs said: "While there is a lower class, I am in it, while there is a criminal element, I am of it, and while there is a soul in prison, I am not free." For a non-exhaustive list of Thurman's use of this quotation, see *PHWT*, 2: 300, 347; 4: 284–85; HT, *The Way of the Mystics*, 16; and HT, *The Greatest of These* (Mills College, CA: Eucalyptus Press, 1944), 25.

Instead, suffusing the idea of democracy for Thurman was, in the words of Vincent Harding, a quest for "a liberating spirituality, a way of exploring and experiencing those crucial life points where personal and societal transformation is creatively joined."[12] It is on the imprecise boundaries of the personal and the social that Thurman's inquiries into democracy are located. How can democratic ideals enhance individual personhood? How can people best express their identities in a social context and how can we create a society in which every individual can flourish? How can a democracy deal with conflicts and its internal contradictions?

Many of the sermons in this book date from a relatively narrow time span, the early 1950s. One main reason for this is technological. Before the advent of tape recording, which in the United States was not commercially available until after World War II, very few of Thurman's sermons were preserved. For the period after 1949 the number of extant sermons and sermon series takes an exponential leap, and this is reflected in the choices for this volume.[13] But there are other reasons. Thurman seems to have been particularly absorbed with general questions about democracy at this time. This was a time of political transition for Thurman and those broadly on the political left, whether formerly sympathetic to the Popular Front or the more progressive aspects of the New Deal, to a much less hospitable time, amid an increasingly all-encompassing and virulent anti-communism. Thurman strongly opposed this tendency, as can be seen in his scorching excoriation of American blood lust after the 1953 execution of Julius and Ethel Rosenberg. And although he always kept his distance from identification with the Communist Party, this did not prevent the FBI from keeping a file on his activities, which included accusations that he "advocated Communism." (These two documents are printed for the first time in the current volume.)[14]

This was also a time of qualified optimism as the campaigns for full Black citizenship, unloosed by the war, increasingly made their weight

---

12. Vincent Harding, foreword to *Jesus and the Disinherited* (1949; repr., Boston: Beacon Press, 1996), xii.

13. See HT, *Moral Struggle and the Prophets*, ed. Peter Eisenstadt and Walter Earl Fluker (Maryknoll, NY: Orbis Books, 2020), xii.

14. See "Howard Thurman's FBI Files," and "Meditation on the Rosenbergs," printed in the current volume.

felt. In April 1948, after delivering the lectures that became *Jesus and the Disinherited* in Austin, Texas, Thurman commented that the South was "still a beknighted [*sic*] part of the world, but I am happy over signs of creative ferment. They seem to be much in evidence."[15] The following year he told the congregation at Fellowship Church that "for some time now" he had wanted to visit Louisiana and Mississippi where "some very important things are happening," and Thurman wanted to "feel it at close hand."[16] Finally, the early Cold War era was a time in which there was much discussion of the nature of American democracy and the role of American democracy in the worldwide struggle against the Soviet Union and communism. If Thurman abhorred the Cold War, he was certainly part of this discussion.[17] In an America that was simultaneously moving forward and backward, it was time for a serious reassessment of the meaning of democracy.

Thurman's writings on democracy collected here are all the more important because, a few crucial exceptions aside, Thurman did not like to give explicitly political sermons or lectures.[18] This was not because he thought politics unimportant, but because, if anything, he thought it too important, with the ever-present danger of its overloading and frying one's emotional circuitry. In a 1938 sermon he spoke of the "thousands and thousands of defenseless men, women, and children" being killed in aerial bombardments in Spain, China, and India and the lives of "sharecroppers in Mississippi and Arkansas." We think, "what a nightmare life must be for those who live always on the threshold of some thing [*sic*] of terror." But Thurman cautioned that "the temptation is to stop with our being outraged," and if not careful, "we will discover that in our outcry and in our anxious indignation we have merely sublimated our impulses to help," and it becomes "less and less likely that we shall go beyond outrage and beyond crying out loud."[19]

---

15. HT to Gretchen Conduitte, April 23, 1948, Folder 21, Box 30, HTC.

16. HT, *Moral Struggle and the Prophets*, 121–22.

17. See, for example, HT, "The Religion of Jesus and the Disinherited," in Thomas Herbert Johnson, ed., *In Defense of Democracy* (New York: Putnam, 1949).

18. Important exceptions, in the years before the sermons in this book commence, include "A 'Native Son' Speaks" (1940), in *PHWT*, 2: 246–52; "The Fascist Masquerade" (1946), in *PHWT*, 3: 145–62.

19. HT, "Kingdom of God" (June 1938), in *PHWT*, 2: 169.

Politics for Thurman was not about the dubious satisfactions of "crying out loud" and cathartic releases of anger. As he wrote in 1938, "always I must be careful lest I become merely aware of [the] world and its needs without being affected by the needs of the world."[20] Wallowing in the headlines for Thurman was a superficial response precisely because it did not involve deep personal reflection or commitment. For Thurman, the question was how an individual, or a group of individuals, can find and muster the inner strength and the outer resolution to embark on a systematic campaign for social transformation, and make the difficult, democracy-sustaining personal commitment to transformative social change possible. This was a searing question that he raised as early as 1927 in a letter to his mentor, Mordecai Wyatt Johnson, seeking how "we may release to the full our greatest spiritual powers, that there may be such a grand swell of spiritual energy that existing systems will be upset from sheer dynamic—and make whatever temporary adjustments as may prove helpful in relieving intolerable situations until there is a genuine uprooting."[21]

Thurman's place in the pantheon of American religious and civic leadership has been widely celebrated since his death in 1981, but what is not so well known about Thurman is that he was also a keen observer and astute interpreter of American democratic dogma. Often caricatured from within and without the African American community as a powerful preacher and detached mystic, until recently Thurman has been ignored, or at best considered irrelevant, to the pressing social issues impacting public life in general—and Black life in particular.[22] His

---

20. HT, "Kingdom of God," 2: 170.

21. See "To Mordecai Wyatt Johnson," September 20, 1927, Oberlin, OH, *PHWT*, 1: 117.

22. Walter E. Fluker, "Walking with God: Preparation, Presence and Practice," https://vimeo.com/298387811, delivered as The Alonzo L. McDonald Lecture, Part I, Candler School of Theology, Emory University, October 23, 2018. See also Walter Earl Fluker, "Leaders Who Have Shaped U.S. Religious Dialogue," in "Howard Thurman: Intercultural and Interreligious Leader," in *Religious Leadership: A Reference Handbook*, vol. 2, ed. Sharon Henderson Callahan (Thousand Oaks, CA: SAGE Publications, 2013), 571–78; and Walter Earl Fluker, "Dangerous Memories and Redemptive Possibilities: Howard Thurman and Black Leadership in the South," in *Black Leaders and Ideologies in the South: Resistance and Non-Violence,* ed. Preston King and Walter Earl Fluker (New York: Taylor & Francis, 2004), 147–76.

approach to social justice issues has been labeled by some as unresponsive to the concrete realities of oppressed peoples. This reading of Thurman, however, is misinformed and unjustified. Any serious, reflective reading of the Thurman corpus reveals a fundamental concern with the plight of the oppressed, and extensive writings on how, through the use of radical nonviolence, their position in society could be altered. Thurman had very clear and strong convictions about African Americans and the nature and destiny of the "national community" and what Sarah Azaransky calls "this worldwide struggle."[23]

Thurman wrote a correspondent in 1937: "My point of interest is religion interpreted against the background of my life and the life of my group in America. I am very much interested in some of the problems that arise in the experience of people who attempt to be Christian in a society that is essentially un-Christian."[24] It was in these years that he was formulating and expounding his distinctively African American conception of radical nonviolence, promoting his idea of the "apostles of sensitiveness," the small cells of activists who would work tirelessly for the transformation of the ills of American society, serving as an inspiration for James Farmer, Pauli Murray, and many others in the first wave of civil rights activism.[25] He told a Black audience in 1932 that "the tragedy of the race is that the idea of being the world's underdog is sinking into his soul," a message in which "the press, magazines, schools and even the church" all "conspir[e] in one grand course to make us think that we are nothing."[26] He told a white audience in 1940 that

> generally speaking the Negro is not a citizen. He is several steps removed from active participation in those social, economic, political arrangements by which our common body politic is controlled. The character of a democracy and the character of those

23. Sarah Azaransky, *This Worldwide Struggle: Religion and the International Roots of the Civil Rights Movement* (New York: Oxford University Press, 2017).

24. HT, "To Ruth Cunningham" (January 18, 1937), in Folder 14, Box 24, HTC.

25. For Thurman on radical nonviolence, see Peter Eisenstadt, *Against the Hounds of Hell* (Charlottesville, VA: University of Virginia Press, 2021), 138–83, 184–96, 244–73. See also Sarah Azaransky's discussion of Thurman's influence on James Farmer and Pauli Murray in *This Worldwide Struggle*, xx–xxx.

26. Eisenstadt, *Against the Hounds of Hell*, 131.

who live in it are determined by the amount of active responsibility felt by and is possible for the individual . . . Responsibility, a free initiative, the sense of the future, these are the things that make for civic character, that make real citizens. These are denied the Negro.[27]

And if he believed in the necessity of a true interracial democracy, he also wrote in 1945, "minority groups are in a unique position . . . [in] keeping alive the true genius of the democratic challenge . . . because minorities are apt to be the most directly and immediately exposed to the effects of the breakdown of the democratic ideals in the body politic."[28]

Thurman has relatively little to say about democracy and Black Americans in the essays from the early 1950s printed in the current volume. In part this is by design. The sermons were all delivered at Fellowship Church; and before white or interracial audiences he was reluctant to speak directly on racial matters. But more generally he wanted his sermons and lectures to encourage his listeners to develop the constructive spiritual power to transform themselves and their society. He felt that Black Americans did not need to be informed about the challenges of being Black, and he did not want his white listeners to come away filled with pity for the plight of the "poor Negro." "If a man feels sorry for you, he can very easily absolve himself from dealing with you in any sense as an equal."[29] Instead, in these sermons he explored the spiritual basis of true democracy, the recognition of what he called the equality of infinite worth, and the need of the dominant group in society to recognize the full "persona" of every individual rather than, as had been the usual practice, reducing Black people to their bodies.

Thurman's corpus is filled with stories and reflections that depict the Black body as *policed*, as a thing that makes sounds, has voice, but cannot speak and feel. In one of his earliest political writings, "'Relaxation' and Race Conflict" (1929), he comments on the historical significance

---

27. "A 'Native Son' Speaks," in *PHWT*, 2: 246–52.

28. HT, "The Cultural and Spiritual Prospect for a Nation Emerging from Total War, in *PHWT*, 3: 107.

29. HT, *Footprints of a Dream: The Story of the Church for the Fellowship of All Peoples* (New York: Harper & Brothers, 1959), 47–48.

of Black subjectivity being relegated to the body as chattel, an object of derision and persecution.

> The slave was essentially a *body*—of course there were many exceptions to this point of view. The idea that the slave was a body has proved itself to be extraordinarily long-lived. As a small boy I remember being stuck with a pin, and when I reacted to it the little [white] boy who had done it said, "Oh, that doesn't hurt you; you can't feel."[30]

The young boy (or girl, he told the story both ways) who stuck Thurman with a pin had merely taken the wisdom of his elders too literally—Black people were incapable of having feelings. But white society as a whole conspired to reduce African Americans to a mere brute, physical presence. Thurman described his time as a Morehouse College undergraduate in the harsh city of Atlanta: "Our physical lives were of little value. Any encounter with a white person was inherently dangerous and frequently fatal. Those of us who managed to remain physically whole found our lives defined in less than human terms."[31]

Thurman did not want to be reduced merely to his Black body, but at the same time, he believed his body and his racial identity were inseparable from his humanity and did not think it a compliment when white friends told him that they never thought of him as Black.[32] Thurman, in his life and his thought, was the epitome of what has been called "colored cosmopolitanism."[33] For Thurman, his experiences with his Black body was a Black person who spoke and felt, and his blackness was inseparable

---

30. *PHWT*, 1: 148 (brackets added). In other places, he refers to a "little girl" who stuck him with her pinafore. See *WHAH*, 11–12.

31. *WHAH*, 36.

32. While in seminary a white friend told him, "I never think of you as a Negro." He told him, "I am a human being, but also a Negro." A 1928 article about Thurman by a white author claimed, somewhat doubtfully, that "this brilliant young Negro wishes to be judged as a man and not as a representative of his race." If he didn't want to be in the position of being a "representative" of all African Americans, Thurman found no contradiction between his human universality and his Black particularity; see Eisenstadt, *Against the Hounds of Hell*, 85, 105.

33. See Nico Slate, *Colored Cosmopolitanism: The Shared Struggle for Freedom in the United States and India* (Cambridge, MA: Harvard University Press, 2012.) See

from his humanity and his understanding of freedom and equality. Thus, it was with a sense of bewilderment and incredulity that he listened to the advice of his major professor, George Cross, who said to his brilliant student toward the end of his last year at Rochester Theological Seminary:

> You are a very sensitive Negro man . . . and doubtless feel under great obligation to put all the weight of your mind and spirit at the disposal of the struggle of your own people for full citizenship. But let me remind you that all social questions are transitory in nature and it would be a terrible waste for you to limit your creative energy to the solution of the race problem, however insistent its nature. Give yourself to the timeless issues of the human spirit . . . Perhaps I have no right to say this to you because as a white man I can never know what it is to be in your situation.[34]

Thurman says that he "pondered the meaning of his words, and wondered what kind of response I could make to this man who did not know that a man and his black skin must face the 'timeless issues of the human spirit' together."[35] This fact of facing the timeless issues of the human spirit in his *Black skin* would become over the years a central question for his conception of a mystical encounter that holds transcendence and Black embodiment in creative tension in the construction of what some scholars call *democratic space*.[36]

---

also Amanda Brown, *The Fellowship Church: Howard Thurman and the Twentieth Century Christian Left* (New York: Oxford University Press, 2021).

34. *WHAH*, 60. Thurman shared this story with Walter Earl Fluker in a conversation in Evanston, Illinois, in April of 1978. The impact of Cross's advice, though not fully realized at that moment, became in time a driving principle for decision making in relation to social action for Thurman. Luther Smith comments on the significance of this occasion and its relation to Thurman's baptism; see Luther E. Smith, *Howard Thurman: The Mystic as Prophet* (Richmond, IN: Friends United Press, 2007), 24.

35. *WHAH*, 60.

36. To live in and out of a Black body, to live as a Black body, to be *Black skin*, connotes what Judith Butler identifies as "boundary, fixity, surface, and intensification," in short, *materiality*; and "it is through the intensification of feeling that bodies and worlds materialize and take shape, or that the effect of boundary, fixity and surface is produced" (Sara Ahmed, "Collective Feelings: Or, the Impressions Left by Others," *Theory, Culture and Society* 21, no. 2 [April 1, 2004]: 29). See also Judith Butler,

For Thurman, walking with God includes the wedding of spirituality and social transformation in the development of democratic space. In
other words, Thurman's imaginative theological project provides a way to
construct possibilities for new spaces, new times, and new rhythms for
historically marginalized and despised bodies within and beyond political constraints and limitations. Therefore, Thurman's understanding of
mystical experience was not a detached otherworldly quest that denied
particularity; rather, particularity—especially individuality, as evidenced
in embodied existence—was, for him, a statement about materiality,
both as a boundary that separates and an arena for affective knowledge,
communication, and agency that bring bodies together.[37]

In his innovative liturgical experiments at the Rankin Chapel of
Howard University, the Fellowship Church in San Francisco, and Marsh
Chapel at Boston University, Thurman explored the efficacy of the body
as a site for communion. Through the arts, music, dance, poetry, ico-
nography, and silence, Thurman sought to create an egalitarian ecclesio-
logical space for interracial, intercultural, and interreligious gatherings
that honored the aesthetic dimensions of the body: *seeing, feeling, smell-
ing, touching, hearing,* and *knowing.*[38] For Thurman, matter *matters,* as

---

Bodies That Matter: On the Discursive Limits of "Sex" (New York: Routledge, 1993),
9. *Democratic space* refers to the ongoing struggle against the reconfiguration of space
and the reordering of time for subjugated bodies. See Jacques Rancière, *Disagreement:
Politics and Philosophy,* trans. Julie Rose (Minneapolis: University of Minnesota
Press, 1999), 29–30; Charles E. Scott, "The Betrayal of Democratic Space," *Journal
of Speculative Philosophy* 22, no. 4 (2008): 304; Jean-Luc Nancy, *The Experience
of Freedom*; and Fluker, "Walking with God: Preparation, Presence and Practice,"
https://vimeo.com/298387811.

37. Fluker, "Walking with God."

38. See Thurman, "A Prayer for Peace," where he speaks of the "smell of life," in
Walter Earl Fluker and Cathy Tumber, eds., *A Strange Freedom: The Best of Howard
Thurman on Religious Life and Public Experience* (Boston: Beacon Press, 1998),
307–8. See also HT, "The Commitment" (March 1949, the Fellowship Church, San
Francisco), in *PHWT,* 3: 309–10. For Thurman, "the Commitment" was not a creed
or a confession of faith but necessary architecture for the church, the building of a
"floor upon which people of . . . radical diversities may stand together." "I mean the
worship of God, the immediate awareness of the pushing out of the barriers of self,
the moment when we flow together into one, when I am not male or female, yellow
or green or black or white or brown, educated or illiterate, rich or poor, sick or well,
righteous or unrighteous—but a naked human spirit that spills over into other human

Luther Smith rightly suggests;[39] indeed, bodies matter, because they dare
to speak, feel, and act. An oft-quoted statement of Thurman underscores
the necessity for the appreciation and embrace of the body's time-space
continuum and human transcendence, that is, being both self-aware and
daring to *live* and *re-narrate* incarnate existence:

> The time and place of a person's life on earth is the time and place
> of the body, but the meaning and significance of that life is as far-
> reaching and redemptive as the gifts, the dedication, the response
> to the demand of the times, the total commitment of one's pow-
> ers can make it.[40]

According to the late Charles Long, Howard Thurman does precisely this work of re-narration of the body and space by resituating "the
problematic [of race] within the structures of inwardness as the locus for
a new rhythm of time," which represents the appropriation of a *mythos*

---

spirits as they spill over into me" (309) . . . "Now, dimension is an aesthetic sense. The
experience of unity in the presence of God, of the oneness of God, puts a scent in my
nostrils that sends me, in all of the things that I do, trying to express it. In my work,
in my relationships with people on the street, I look with new eyes on those with
reference to whom, when I was imprisoned in my little narrow self, I had no experience
of oneness. The fears that I had, that kept eating away at the basis of social security, are
now removed, because I have let down my guard in an effort to move creatively into an
understanding of other people and let them move creatively into an understanding of
me. And in that moment of shuttling, they become a part of me forever" (310).

39. Luther E. Smith, "Intimate Mystery: Howard Thurman's Search for Alternative Meaning," in *Ultimate Reality and Meaning* 11, no. 2 (June 1988): 97. The
notions of *living* in Black skin and the *policing* of the Black body find affinity with
Willie James Jennings's argument that Europeans, in their colonial conquests,
performed "a deeply theological act that mirrored the identity and action of God in
creating," in which they transitioned and reconfigured land and territory as part of the
domain of the project of whiteness. Jennings adds, "Theorists and theories of race will
not touch the ground until they reckon with the foundations of racial imaginings in
the deployment of an altered theological vision of creation. We must narrate not only
the alteration of bodies, but of space itself." See Willie James Jennings, *The Christian
Imagination: Theology and the Origins of Race* (New Haven, CT: Yale University Press,
2010), 60; and Walter Earl Fluker, "The Politics of Conversion and the Civilization
of Friday," in *The Courage to Hope: From Black Suffering to Human Redemption,*" ed.
Quinton Dixie and Cornel West (Boston: Beacon Press, 1999).

40. *WHAH,* 208.

that provided meaning and affirmation of human dignity to an otherwise hopeless existence.[41]

Thurman's experimentation with contested democratic space grows out of a long history of resisting chattel slavery, Jim Crow, segregation, and the terror of the rope. Therefore, while his notion of democracy references historical documents like the Declaration of Independence, the Constitution of the United States, and the Emancipation Proclamation, one cannot assume that democratic space for Thurman was the same as it was for the American founding fathers or European intellectuals and *philosophes*.[42] Democratic space, for Thurman, demonstrates both the claiming of the right and the moral duty to dissent, to disagree based on the radical freedom and the inherent dignity and worth of the individual within the context of Black suffering. Thurman's religious and ethical moorings, therefore, are both an imaginative conjuring of sequestered space and a demand for the reconfiguration of history and memory that rests in a return to and re-narration of creation and the reclaiming of the body as sacred space.[43] For Thurman, this is not a journey into an Edenic paradise of puritanical innocence; rather it is a perilous pilgrimage into the interiority of religious experience and the exteriority of democratic landscapes witnessed in bodily existence and time, or, what he called in

---

41. Charles Long writes, "The slaves who lived both within and outside of history, created historical structures but having no power to determine the locus of their meaning found a spiritual locus outside the body of historical time in which to save their bodies and to give meaning to their communities. The spirituals were their myths, and as Ashis Nandy put it, the 'affirmation of ahistoricity is an affirmation of the dignity and autonomy of the non-modern, [non-Western] peoples'" (Charles H. Long, "Howard Thurman and the Meaning of Religion in America," in Mozella G. Mitchell, ed., *The Human Search: Howard Thurman and the Quest for Freedom, Proceedings of the Second Annual Thurman Convocation* [New York: Peter Lang, 1992], 141) (brackets in original).

42. Benjamin Isakhan, "Eurocentrism and the History of Democracy," in *Politische Vierteljahresschrift* 51 (2016): 56–70.

43. See HT, *The Search for Common Ground* (New York: Harper & Row, 1971), 5. His central question is, "What is there that seems to be implicit, or inherent in [human] racial memory that is on the side of community?" (brackets added). See also his Convocation Address, in *Perspectives, A Journal of Pittsburgh Theological Seminary* 13, no. 2 (Spring 1972), and his Mendenhall Lecture "Community and the Will of God" (February 1961), HTC.

his 1945 essay, "the inner life and world-mindedness."[44] Therefore, it is not sufficient simply to focus on the inner life without being aware and engaged in the complex social, political, and economic arrangements that order and structure the individual's embodied existence, which for him, was necessary for the task of creating democratic space.

Thurman's four sermons on the Declaration of Independence, the centerpiece of this volume, are a link in a long historical chain of African Americans grappling with the promise of this document as well as its hypocrisies. This began as early as 1776, when Lemuel Haynes, a free Black man from Massachusetts, subsequently a New England Congregational minister, wrote an essay, "Liberty Further Extended: Or Free Thoughts on the Illegality of Slave-Keeping," that had as its epigraph the newly written preamble of the Declaration on the inalienable rights to life and liberty. In his essay, Haynes stated that "Liberty is a Jewel which was handed Down to Man from the Cabinet of Heaven, and is Coeval with Existence."[45] Thurman expressed himself in different words, but he was fully in agreement with this perhaps most basic tenet of Afro-Christianity, that Christianity is a religion of liberty and liberation. For Thurman, Thomas Jefferson's original vision of democracy was fatally flawed because of its emphasis on private property as a basic right. "When property becomes sacred," Thurman had written, people are reduced to expendable things, and a slave society is only the highest and most com-

44. "The Inner Life and World-Mindedness," Thurman Papers, Boston University, *PHWT*, 3: 108–13. The "sense of self" is rooted in the nature of the self. Thurman makes a distinction between the inner and outer dimensions of the self. For him, the individual is both a child of nature and a child of spirit. The outer dimension of the self is part of the external world of nature. See HT, *The Creative Encounter*, p. 19; HT, *Disciplines*, p. 57; and HT, *Search for Common Ground*, 21.

45. Haynes never published his anti-slavery essay. It was discovered only in the 1980s; see Ruth Bogin, "'Liberty Further Extended': A 1776 Antislavery Manuscript by Lemuel Haynes," *William and Mary Quarterly* 3rd series, 40, no. 1 (1983): 85–105. For Haynes, see John Saillant, *Black Puritan, Black Republican: The Life and Thought of Lemuel Haynes, 1753–1833* (New York: Oxford University Press, 2002.) For the African American identification and argument with the Declaration, see Mia Bay, "See Your Declaration Americans!!!: Abolitionism, Americanism, and the Revolutionary Tradition in Free Black Politics," in Michael Kazin and Joseph A. McCartin, eds., *Americanism: New Perspectives on the History of an Idea* (Chapel Hill: University of North Carolina Press, 2006), 25–52.

plete realization of a society built on the preservation of private property in things. Private property then becomes an extension of oneself and one's life, and to protect their property "men are held guiltless when they destroy life that threatens their own life."[46]

But Thurman did not believe that Jefferson's crabbed view of democracy exhausted the meanings of the Declaration. The only real basis for democracy was recognizing what he liked to call the "infinite worth" of every individual, not treating persons as means to an end, and creating societal structures that would advance those goals, and rejecting what he called the "cult of inequality," the belief that without a rigidly enforced hierarchy, society would dissolve into chaos.[47]

This was a revolutionary idea, and Thurman in the 1950s and 1960s saw revolutions sprouting everywhere.[48] In 1955, speaking of independence movements in Asia and Africa, he quoted another part of the preamble to the Declaration: "Governments are instituted among men, deriving their powers from the consent of the governed; That whenever any form of government becomes destructive of these ends, it is the Right of the People to alter and abolish it."[49] Within a few years Thurman was writing enthusiastically of another revolution, what in 1963 he called the "profound social revolution that is taking place particularly in the United States, one which involves the future of the relationships between black and white citizens of the land."[50] This was a realization of Thurman's idea of loyalty, as he discussed in 1951, as "the willing and steadfast and practical devotion of a person to a cause," enmeshing one's fate with that of others. In Thurman's words, loyalty is "essentially a spiritual phenomenon

---

46. HT, "The Significance of Jesus III: Love" (September 1937), in *PHWT*, 2: 64. "That upon which [a person] depends as a guarantee of his economic survival becomes an extension of himself. It becomes his private property, and any individual who threatens to disturb his security threatens his life." Therefore, writing of contemporary labor violence, "hence, men feel quite justified in importing gunmen or thugs to kill defenseless strikers in a factory."

47. See "America in Search of a Soul," printed in the current volume. The "cult of inequality" was a favorite phrase of Thurman; see *PHWT*, 4:113, 120n6, 218.

48. For Thurman on revolution, see HT, "Religious Faith and Revolution," printed in the current volume, and Eisenstadt, *Against the Hounds of Hell*, 317.

49. HT, "Speech at Lambda Kappa Mu Human Relations Award Dinner" (November 1955), in *PHWT*, 4: 131–36.

50. Eisenstadt, *Against the Hounds of Hell*, 317.

derived from the nature of the universe," the "fusing of the outer and the inner," loyalty to oneself and to one's chosen community, to one's comrades.[51]

He had written in 1950 that "always in revolution there is this sense of the collective destiny, a sense of me-too-ness with reference to other people. I am not alone—that is what it says, and that becomes a part of the dynamic of every revolution."[52] A decade later, he found himself within this transforming, revolutionary sense of loyalty.[53] "Perhaps the most significant thing that has happened in the last few stirring years of the vast struggle for civil rights in the South and the North has been the dramatic loss of fear on the part of the masses of Negroes," with "the sense of direct, conscious, and collective participation in a joint destiny," generating "a strange and wonderful courage."[54] It was this sort of loyalty to liberty and freedom that Thurman experienced, when, part of the throng, he participated in the March on Washington that August: "Nothing like this has ever happened in the history of our country. I was one of 200,000 people sharing a moment that contained all time and all experience, when everything was moving and everything was standing still, a moment that had in it the stillness of absolute motion."[55] It was also perhaps the culminating moment for Thurman of his idea of nonviolent revolution. As he argued in the 1961 sermon, "Emancipation and Human Freedom," a basic premise of the civil rights revolution was the determination that life is not "essentially finished, fixed, set, frozen," but "is essentially fluid, dynamic, creative."[56] For Thurman, this was being demonstrated at every rally, demonstration, sit-in, and freedom ride, melting a social system that too many for too long had believed to be rock-hard, solid, and unchangeable.

The civil rights revolution in the mid-1960s intersected with a movement for Black nationalism. Thurman was always supportive of Black self-assertion, proud of his own racial identity, but he did not want his Blackness

---

51. HT, "The Meaning of Loyalty I," printed in the current volume.

52. HT, "Religious Faith and Revolution," printed in the current volume.

53. For Thurman's many instances of comparing the civil rights movement to a revolution, see Eisenstadt, *Against the Hounds of Hell*, 317–18.

54. HT, "Nonviolence and the Art of Reconciliation," in *PHWT*, 5: 7.

55. Eisenstadt, *Against the Hounds of Hell*, 319–20.

56. HT, "Emancipation and Human Freedom," printed in the current volume.

defined too rigidly, or defined for him, as can be seen in the 1972 sermon "Black Pentecost: Footprints of the Disinherited." "An absolute is an absolute, and it is the nature of an absolute to be an absolute, and I have a built-in allergy to any social absolute, because it is the absolute in white society that has lacerated me, and the only thing an absolute knows what to do is to absolute."[57] Thurman believed personal and group identity was an open door and not a wall. As he stated twenty years earlier in a sermon on "Democracy and the Individual," printed in the current volume, the central problem of democracy is that of the "urgency and the necessity constantly to redefine the boundaries of the group. Because if I do not redefine the boundaries of the group increasingly so as to include more and more diversity, more and more differences, more and more radically alien backgrounds and orientations, then the genius of democracy itself, rooted in this spiritual relationship, becomes a device that makes for group arrogance and group superiority."[58]

The final sermon in this book is a bicentennial sermon from 1976, "America in Search of a Soul," and it serves as a culmination and a recapitulation of many of the earlier sermons in this volume. In it, Thurman elaborates on his distinction between freedom and liberty. Liberty is social and political. "It can be given; it can be taken away. It can be wiped out." Freedom "is the process by which, standing in my place where I am, I can so act in that place as to influence, order, alter, or change the future." Freedom can be latent. It is "the sense of option." You might not have the liberty to exercise that option. But no one can reach inside you and force you to stop thinking of an alternative way of living your life, unless you let them."

This contrast between freedom and liberty, Thurman argues, is a key, and a key contradiction in American history, a country founded on liberty and freedom, and a country that, from its creation, suppressed the freedom and liberties of the indigenous population, of other racial minorities, and those condemned to slavery. Perhaps more than any other of his sermons or essays, "America in Search of a Soul" shows Thurman's bifurcated views of America and of American democracy. He saw the

---

57. HT, "Black Pentecost."

58. HT, "A Faith to Live By: Democracy and the Individual II," printed in the current volume.

creation of the United States as a great experiment, which he describes in almost providential terms, a test to see if people of very different backgrounds and levels of power could create a society of true equals. America for Thurman is a school, God's school, a school to test whether the promises of the Declaration of Independence, the Gettysburg Address, the Letter from Birmingham Jail, and other exalted symbolic documents are more than mere words. God has been an only moderately effective teacher because "Now, school is out. School is out, and it's been out for some time."[59] Some lessons have been learned, some lessons were never learned, and some lessons have been unlearned. If Thurman believed America was founded on a contradiction, he also believed, as one of his core religious and political beliefs, that no contradiction, regardless of how fixed and adamantine it might appear, was ever final.

This introduction opened with the quote, "Don't ask yourself what the world needs. Ask yourself what makes you come alive, and go do that, because what the world needs is people who have come alive." It also was so, and almost certainly more important for Thurman. The world cannot tell you what makes you come alive. "My life is rooted in a kind of awareness of my meaning that does not arise from your interpretation of my significance, that nothing, that no judgment that you impose upon me, no order of society into which you seek to have me regimented, can sever my roots from the dimension of awareness that gives to me my inner significance."[60] Both sentiments are part of Thurman's vision of democratic space, a community in which everyone is both infinitely equal and infinitely unique. "I have always wanted to be *me* without making it difficult for you to be *you*," he wrote in the preface to *The Search for Common*

---

59. HT, "America in Search of a Soul." Thurman used the same metaphor in "A Faith to Live By: Democracy and the Individual I," printed in the current volume: "We have been sent to school by Life, by God to develop confidence and faith, technique, methodologies for implementing the dream of one world, one family that God has for the human race. And school is out, school is out and there isn't enough time to do any teaching now. There is just time enough left for contagion. Either we demonstrate or die. There is no alternative left and I wonder what God thinks about his students, I wonder."

60. HT, "The Declaration of Independence I: Created Equal," printed in the current volume.

Ground.[61] When Thurman was dying, in early 1981, he told his wife, Sue Bailey Thurman, "It is wonderful that you did not come between me and my struggle. You did not stand in my way."[62] In Thurman's ideal democratic space, people would learn to care, nurture, and love one another enough to let them grow, and to not stand in their way.

Thurman never lived in an ideal democratic space, and he never expected to. Neither should we. In 1946, in one of his most trenchant political essays, "The Fascist Masquerade," he explored how American fascism hid and festered behind the facades of intolerant brands of "true Christianity or true Americanism . . . provid[ing] for a legitimizing of sadistic or demonical impulses." American fascism had many hatreds—of Jews, foreigners and immigrants, organized labor, liberals and radicals—and relied especially on the "appeal to anti-Negro sentiment in many sections, communities and among many groups." This "is a 'natural' for the would-be demagogue. It is sure fire." Fascism hates anyone and everyone who does not fit into their narrow vision of what it means to be Christian and what it means to be American.[63]

For all that changed since Thurman wrote "The Fascist Masquerade," too much, far too much, has not. Bigotry is still "sure fire." As this is being written, at the end of 2021, we are all still living in circumstances very far from Thurman's ideal democratic space. Two years into a debilitating pandemic, our worries about the future of democracy in the United States and overseas, along with a host of other problems that seem increasingly out of reach of democratic solutions have become acute. Thurman might have been dismayed by our current situation, but he would not have been surprised. His was a politics that was long practiced in the art of spiritual survival in inhospitable places and times. The first task was to "take the responsibility for how, mark my word, *how* I react to the forces that impinge upon my life, forces that are not responsive to my will, my desire, my ambition, my dream, my hope—forces that don't know that

---

61. HT, *The Search for Common Ground,* xii.

62. Sue Bailey Thurman, Memorial Tribute, "Simmering on the Calm Presence and Profound Wisdom of Howard Thurman," special issue, *Debate & Understanding,* ed. Ricardo A. Millet and Conley H. Hughes (Spring 1982), 91.

63. HT, "The Fascist Masquerade," in *PHWT,* 3:145–62.

I'm here."[64] Giving way to unreasonable fear or giving up to despair were never options, according to Thurman. The second task, following an honest appraisal of one's situation, was to do what one could to change it.

In one of his meditations, Thurman references Martin Buber, who said that life for him was at its very best when he was living on what he called "the narrow ridge." It is a way of life that generates zest for each day's round because it is lived between abysses on either side with anticipation and imagination that gives us wings. "In each of us," Thurman writes, "there is a 'Cascade Eagle,' a bird that is higher when soaring the [narrow] gorge than the highest soarer above the plains—because the gorge is in the mountains. To give this eagle wings is the call to every *person*."[65] Democracy will always inhabit the narrow ridge between what is possible and what is impossible. If impossibility seems to have gained the upper hand in recent years, we can only push back against it with renewed strength, knowing that our freedoms will always be measured in part by the resistance it engenders from the unfreedoms around us. Or in Thurman's words, "It is in reference to the relationship between the movable and that which at the moment seems to be immovable that I get the sense of play which is freedom."[66] He loved the Declaration of Independence, despite some of the flaws of its creators, because he knew that democracy always had to be revolutionary, capable of renewing itself, capacious in its sympathies, willing to defend its fragility against its enemies, and, above all, an affirmation of the aliveness of life.[67]

---

64. HT, "America in Search of a Soul."

65. "The Narrow Ridge," in HT, *The Inward Journey* (New York: Harper & Row, 1961), 85–86. Martin Buber (1878–1965) was a German-Israeli philosopher, religious thinker, and social theorist. The description of the Cascade eagle was taken from Herman Melville's *Moby-Dick*, where it is called a "Catskill eagle"; see HT, *Moral Struggle and the Prophets* (Maryknoll, NY: Orbis Books, 2020), 92n14.

66. HT, "The Declaration of Independence III: Liberty," printed in the current volume.

67. See HT, "The Declaration of Independence II: Life—An Inalienable Right," printed in the current volume.

Religious Faith and Revolution

July 1, 1950
Fellowship Church

What is a revolution? What is its connection to religious faith? This sermon provides Thurman's most searching answers to these questions. For Thurman, "always there is present in revolution the wrestle of the individual with some form of tyranny," and if the tyranny is "of such intensity and endures over a time interval of sufficient extension, all of the life dies, and the moment for revolution passes." Revolutions take place when people refuse to be defeated by tyranny, when "some kind of belief, some kind of faith, yes, some kind of transcendent faith . . . becomes the basis, the incentive, for integrated action." And as a consequence, "individuals reject one way, one pattern of living, and seek to substitute for that which is rejected another way of life, which way of life is to the revolutionary more satisfying, more fulfilling, more significant than the previous way of life." When enough like-minded feel and act together in this way, there can be a revolution.

In this sermon, delivered a few days before the Fourth of July, Thurman speaks of the American Revolution, as well as of the non-violent revolution of Gandhi. What they had in common, Thurman argues, was a willingness to sacrifice for the whole, including, in extreme circumstances, one's own life. And this is because "always in revolution there is this sense of the collective destiny, a sense of me-too-ness with reference to other people."

Thurman is also alert to the negative possibilities of revolutions. They can become inflexible, imposing their standards on everyone, and excluding no one from its scope. Speaking of the Bolshevik revolution of 1917, he argued that "the logic of revolution is that it must become worldwide." (Unreferenced by Thurman, but certainly on his mind and that of his congregation, were the events of the previous week, when on June 25, 1950, North Korea, backed by the Soviet Union, sent its troops across the 38th Parallel, the precipitating event of the Korean War.)

1

The most provocative aspect of the sermon is Thurman's claim that "there is always in revolution, even bad revolutions, the elements, the same elements, that we find in religion," which for Thurman is a commitment to an all-encompassing, all-involving faith, with all that implies, for better and for worse. Religion, he argues, operates on two levels. There is the "intimate and personal and private element of devotion," which provides a way to live in dignity, whatever the circumstances. And then there is the sort of religion that "operates as a force that lays hold upon you," takes over your life, propelling you to ends "that are non-personal and non-private," toward ends that are in some way revolutionary. Thurman appreciates both kinds of religion, and sees both as a necessary component of a full religious life. The difference between revolutionary faith and religious faith is that revolutionary faith must be judged and adjusted to the possibility of its realization. Religious faith is less constrained by pragmatic considerations. If one's faith seems to be, in terms of worldly success, a failure, this "does not relieve the religious man of his responsibility of continuing to affirm it."

Nonetheless, Thurman is convinced that "every religious man stands in immediate candidacy to be a revolutionary, and every revolutionary in the last analysis draws upon the same springs of vitality and strength and energy that is the ground and the fulfillment of religion." In the background of this sermon, and of many of the sermons in this volume, is the possibility that Black Americans, through a still largely inchoate mix of religious faith and revolution, will collectively overthrow their oppressors and their oppression.

MEDITATION

How deep is our need. How deep is our need. We bring, each one of us, our little world, our little world with all of its tensities, the difficulties with which we cannot deal, the agonies for which there seems to be no balm, the chaos for which there seems to be no order—our little world, with its joys, some unspeakable, intimate, and precious, its hopes unrealized, and that stand always on the horizon beckoning us—our little world. We bring them, Our Father, to thee. Our little worlds are in the midst of other worlds, other worlds that impinge upon our world and push it out of shape, squeeze it and mash it, the great world of impersonal event and destiny, and yet always it comes back to our little world. We all of us bare ourselves before thee, Our Father, seeking only that we be understood, Our Father, that's all; even in the midst of what we must suffer, if we are understood, O God, Our Father, that is enough to provide the strength we need to carry on. Balm of hurt minds, finder of lost spirits, redeemer of sinners, be near us, O God, and bless our moments. Amen.

Today I am faced with the kind of dilemma or difficulty that I have not experienced during the entire six years—six years next Sunday incidentally—that we have been at work here with the church, and that is why it has been impossible for my mind and my spirit to get their hands on what I seek. So, it would be very simple if we could convert this into one large discussion and gather from you answers to certain questions in my mind, which answers would inspire reactions again, and together we might find it a most profitable hour. What we shall do, nevertheless, is work at the thing that I am trying to find and, perhaps, at the end my sense of failure will be as marked as it is now with this difference: you will share the responsibility because you are participants in this process.

I will begin then with the correction—perhaps this will be more helpful with the thing for which I am feeling: instead of using the word "religion" I want to use the terms "religious faith" and revolution.

The first thing that is significant in our reflection is that revolution as an individual experience and as a social experience has much in it that is common with religion, and religion as a personal experience and as a social experience. Revolution takes place when individuals reject one way, one pattern of living, and seek to substitute for that which is rejected another way of life, which way of life is to the revolutionary more satisfying, more fulfilling, more significant that the previous way of life. Always there is present in revolution the wrestle of the individual with some form of tyranny, some pressure that is put down upon the individual, which pressure becomes increasingly unbearable; and, if the individuals who are subjected to the pressure are able to keep this pressure from robbing them of all feeling—mark this—then the chances of change are possible. But if the pressure succeeds in destroying all sensitiveness, all feeling, then revolution is not possible. There is a timetable here. I remember some years ago reading about a lady who went to visit Dr. Locke—she was writing for the *Woman's Home Companion*; she observed his treatment of people.[1] She noticed that in the little chair under the tree in which all the patients sat, and the doctor sat in front while he manipulated their feet—you know something about the method—a little crippled girl sat in the chair. The doctor took her shoe off and did something to her foot and then gave it a quick twist, and the little girl screamed. A shudder went over all the people who were waiting. The lady who wrote the article said that in the afternoon she met the little girl's father down at the village post office. She expressed her sympathy, and the father said, "I appreciate how you feel, but there is one little thing that you don't understand. You see, when our daughter first came here weeks ago the doctor could do anything to her foot and she couldn't feel it. When I heard her scream this afternoon, I said, "Thank God! Life is in that foot at last."

Now if the pressure, the tyranny, is of such intensity and endures over a time interval of sufficient extension, all of the life dies, and the moment for revolution passes. Before revolution can take place in a situation of that sort, new nerves must be grown, and men who have worked as revolutionaries in situations in which all of the life, all of the quickness, has disappeared have spent their time way down in the darkness patching nerve ends.

Now there is something else about it. There is always in revolution some kind of belief, some kind of faith, yes, some kind of transcendent faith, which faith becomes what? Becomes the basis, the incentive, for integrated action. It may be a dream, it may be some other kind of world order that is personified that becomes the point, the center of focus, but whatever it may be always wherever there is a revolution there is the response of the individual or the individuals to some transcendent concept, something in the light of which all other judgments of life take place. All over

---

1. William Locke (1880–1942) was a Canadian physician whose unorthodox method of treating arthritis and other ailments through foot and toe manipulation received a good deal of attention in the 1930s, including by Thurman; see *PHWT*, 2: 252n2. In 1940 Thurman cited Locke, in a similar fashion, in the context of the African American response to white racist attacks after World War I, which expressed itself "in wild resentment expressing itself in rioting, etc. . . . This rioting was a sign of life, of an awakening citizenship"; HT, *PHWT*, 2: 250. The *Women's Home Companion* was a monthly magazine published between 1873 and 1957.

the United States today many people are celebrating the American Revolution—we don't remember that we were pushed off on this whole sea by
revolution, and that the men whom we call our Founding Fathers were
revolutionaries, and the Father of Our Country was a revolutionary. They
were responding to a transcendent idea, couched in interesting terms.
We have it broken down to what we call the Constitution, and the Bill
of Rights, and all sorts of other things, but it was a new way of life that
took a form that was personalized, and in response to it they were willing to do the second thing that is always true in revolutions, and that is
to surrender one's possessions, including one's life. It inspires surrender;
they actually went out in the seventeenth and eighteenth centuries with
pitchforks and with clubs, a very irrational procedure, against bullets. But
that was all right; the most precious thing that they had, they surrendered
it without pressure, except the pressure of the relationship to the thing,
so always then there is present in revolution commitment. The curiously
interesting thing about revolution at this point is that the commitment
becomes increasingly an absolute commitment, a commitment that is so
demanding upon the personality that the commitment becomes the basis
of all ethical behavior. "That is right." "That is wrong." Right and wrong
are interpreted in terms of the bearing that this particular deed will have
upon the integrity of the commitment. Very interesting, isn't it?

Not only that, but there is a third thing and a fourth thing. Always in
revolution there is this sense of the collective destiny, a sense of me-too-
ness with reference to other people. I am not alone—that is what it says,
and that becomes a part of the dynamic of every revolution. The revolution that Mr. Gandhi carried on in India, a non-violent revolution—
when they were disciplining the people to face the British army without
violence they had their hospital stretchers and their orderlies—the whole
thing was to be prepared to take care of the casualties. The advice that
Mr. Gandhi gave them was that when this group is mowed down there
will be more to take their place because every time you see one, you see
the host, and each one then has the sense of sharing in a collective destiny
and his little life becomes irrelevant, really, in terms of his being able,
wishing to [hold on?] to it, and for its sake sacrifice [for] the whole.[2] But

2. Thurman met Mahatma Gandhi, the leader of the Indian independence
movement, in India in February 1936, and wrote extensively about him; see HT,

he finds the fulfillment, the redemption of his little life, in the collective destiny of his fellows. That is why there is always in revolution, even bad revolution, the same elements that we find in religion.

Let us look at that for a moment. Religion operates, it seems to me, in human life at two levels. There is that intimate and personal and private element of devotion when the individual as an individual seeks to establish within himself some measure of equilibrium and calmness and peace. This aspect of religion is private and intimate and personal. It is characterized by devotion, by prayer, by meditation, by certain rites private in character. It is something that the individual seeks for himself, a kind of personal assurance in order that he may live his personal life, his private life, with meaning and with dignity and thereby be able to withstand the forces and the pressures that move upon him from the outside and seek to twist him and embitter him and push him out of shape. Always somewhere in the quiet places of his spirit he has his little altar before which he kneels and there get his little soul recharged, lifted, strengthened, his personal sins forgiven, his life oriented, his judgments purified, his desires cleansed. That is one aspect, and everybody has that. Don't forget it. Whatever may be the loud things you say to the contrary, everybody has that.

Now religion operates in another way. It operates as a force that lays hold upon you. Remember that in the other way it is something that you are seeking, a kind of digging your well to get the water that you might drink and be refreshed so that you can make your journey from here to there. This other sense is one when you are possessed. You are laid hold upon. Something takes charge of you. When you feel its grasp upon your spirit you surrender, and when you surrender then at once you become involved in the ends that religion seeks that are non-personal and non-private. Now those ends are dependent upon a lot of things. Let us take an illustration. Take a religious group like the Jehovah's Witnesses, just a case in point, and always when I refer to any religious group I do so with reverence. As long as the Jehovah's Witnesses are involved in the first

"Mahatma Gandhi," in *The Way of the Mystics* (Maryknoll, NY: Orbis Books, 2021), 54–61; and Quinton Dixie and Peter Eisenstadt, *Visions of a Better World: Howard Thurman's Pilgrimage to India and the Origins of African American Radical Nonviolence* (Boston: Beacon Press, 2011).

aspect of religion, the private, intimate, personal, they are never arrested. There is no conflict. But when in the midst of that experience they are laid hold upon by what seems to them to be a transcendent power, then they must do something; and when they start doing something they inform their deeds with their religious experience and not only their religious experience but their religious interpretation, so if it is during a time of war they get into trouble. Over and over again our courts have dealt with the problems of religious liberty, etc., involving this remarkable group of people, whatever you may think of them.[3] The distinction between these two aspects of religion had to be made clear. Therefore, when religion becomes that which has possessed an individual there is no way by which you can determine what that individual will do. There is no way. And there is no power in heaven or hell that can stop him. You can do all sorts of things but you can't stop him because, you see, he feels that when he has felt this and has surrendered to it, he has surrendered to it, his mind, his money, his life, everything, his ideas. Often you surrender your ideas without changing them; you surrender your ideas and then you start to work them out, and the fact that you have had this religious experience has simply put you in a stronger and more powerful position to carry out your little idea. Do you see what I am saying?

Now let us push it just a little further. There is always a sense of sharing a collective destiny. That is why as soon as religion moves from the first aspect to the second, the element that we call the missionary element begins to appear. It takes many forms. Sometimes it is just going out, actually beating the bushes. Often it is merely standing on the dignity of one's experience, looking with measured contempt at those who

---

3. Jehovah's Witnesses, an Adventist, millenarian Christian denomination, founded in 1870, adopting its current name in 1931, has frequently figured in free speech and free exercise of religion cases because of the refusal of its members to serve in the armed forces or recognize the symbols of the American government. In 1943, in West Virginia State Board of Elections v. Barnette, the U.S. Supreme Court ruled that the refusal of members of the denomination to salute the flag was not grounds for expulsion from school, overruling a decision by the court only three years earlier. Thurman strongly disagreed with the theology of the Jehovah's Witnesses, but admired them because their single-minded focus on salvation and making converts led them to abandon the standard segregationist Protestant proprieties. See Eisenstadt, *Against the Hounds of Hell,* 190.

have not been laid hold upon by the secret. In the last analysis there is always this feeling for a sense of collective destiny, the thing that is in the mind of that which has laid hold upon us with reference to which we are instrumental. [This] also includes first those that are nearest and closest to us, those who are involved in the same kind of dilemma, same kind of difficulty, same kind of pressure, same kind of frustration, and then little by little the horizon broadens just as it does in revolution. At first the revolution has in mind this collective destiny merely for those who are immediately under the direct tyranny. Then after a while the basis gets broader and broader. We see that this has happened in the Russian Revolution. The logic of revolution is that it must become worldwide. That is the magic of it, for this insistence that I have found as of major moment and significance for me must at last be made available for all the human beings everywhere. If there is no ready-made pressure that would create it, then the revolutionary must of necessity read into the patterns of life, the tyranny. For it must be there in order that there will be a sound rationale for the fulfillment of the logic of revolution. The same thing is true about religion. Once a man feels that he has been touched and there comes into his life a new glory and a fresh orientation as to its meaning and its possibilities, this thing of infinitely great significance to him cannot be enjoyed merely by him. It must be enjoyed by the people whom he likes, and then by the people who are liked by them, and then by the people who have the same kind of clothes that he wears, and then by the people who have different clothes, for if they had this thing they would wear clothes like mine, and on and on. Finally, you see, the whole world becomes involved in this business.

Now, and finally I am through, that is, I am stopping, the difference between revolution and religion: One difference, as I see it, religion has always in it an ethical quality, and here you may rejoice to disagree; it has in it an ethical quality that extends beyond the relationship of this quality to the survival of the religion. I will say it again. There is present always in religion an ethical quality, which ethical quality is binding in itself, without regard to whether or not the response to this quality is satisfactory as in accordance with the immediate demands of religion. In other words, value judgments in religion are intrinsic, are important, are significant, are supremely important, whether or not in the life expression of the religion, the value judgment makes sense. That is why many people say they cannot be intelligent and be religious, for we always want in our experience [that] our ethical concerns will find validation. We want to feel, you see, that the world as I live in it yields always a possibility that the thing in which I believe with all my heart as being true and right will work in the world. That is one insistence. Now reach it and we shall go on together. It is a peculiar rationality of religion that even as it insists upon the workability of its insight, even as it insists upon what may be called the empirical validation of its insight, yet if it doesn't work that does not relieve the religious man of his responsibility of continuing to affirm it. That is the difference. That is it. So, the prophet Habakkuk says, For though there be no sheep in the stall, though there be no grapes on the vine, though there be no figs on the fig-tree, nevertheless, I will continue to affirm.[4]

With revolution always the test of the concept, the test of the ethical judgment, the test of the moral judgment, is the bearing that it has on the workability of the fulfillment of the ideals of the revolution. Therefore, every religious man stands in immediate candidacy to be a revolutionary, and every revolutionary in the last analysis draws upon the same springs of vitality and strength and energy that is the ground and the fulfillment of religion.

4. Habakkuk 3:17. In 1950 Thurman completed a commentary on Habakkuk for *The Interpreter's Bible*, though it was not published until 1956. For its background and the text of the commentary, see *PHWT*, 4: 136–50.

The Meaning of Loyalty I

May 6, 1951
Fellowship Church

In 1951, in the United States, and especially in California, the word "loyalty" was much on people's minds. In 1950 the state passed the Levering Act, requiring all state employees to sign a so-called loyalty oath, requiring them to avow that they were not a member of the Communist Party nor otherwise believed in the "overthrow of the United States Government." In August 1950 thirty-one University of California faculty members were fired for their failure to sign the oath; others resigned in protest.[1] Fellowship Church opposed the California loyalty oaths, and it was a likely inspiration for the six sermons Thurman delivered on loyalty in the summer of 1951.[2] Typically, Thurman did not discuss, except obliquely, the immediate political question of loyalty oaths, instead exploring and attempting to rehabilitate the idea of loyalty. From the six sermons Thurman delivered on loyalty in 1951, the editors are not publishing the final three, on Job and Second Isaiah, topics covered elsewhere in the sermon series volumes.[3]

In this sermon series, and especially this sermon, Thurman makes reference to and use of the work of the American philosopher Josiah Royce (1855–1916), whose The Philosophy of Loyalty *(1908) was the preeminent English-language work on loyalty.[4] Although Thurman had been familiar*

---

1. See Bob Blauner, *Resisting McCarthyism: To Sign or Not Sign California's Loyalty Oath* (Palo Alto, CA: Stanford University Press, 2009).

2. For the church's opposition to loyalty oaths, see HT, *Footprints of a Dream: The Story of the Church for the Fellowship of All Peoples* (New York: Harper & Brothers, 1959), 115.

3. See Howard Thurman, *Moral Struggle and the Prophets*, ed. Peter Eisenstadt and Walter Earl Fluker (Maryknoll, NY: Orbis Books, 2020), 19–29, 59–65.

4. Josiah Royce, *The Philosophy of Loyalty* (New York: Macmillan, 1908). Royce was a native Californian who graduated from the recently established University

with Royce for a number of years, there are few references to Royce in his earlier work, although there are certainly similarities in their thought. For Royce, loyalty is a matter of volition. Loyalty cannot be imposed or obliged; it can only be chosen, freely. At the same time, we can only live our loyalties within the context of our lives, with loyalties to others, to the loyalties that bind us into communities (Royce was the one who coined the phrase "beloved community"), and, ultimately, to the inherent structures of the universe itself. Loyalty to good causes enhances those ties. Loyalty to bad causes does not. For Royce, "a cause is good, not only for me, but for mankind, in so far as it is essentially a loyalty to loyalty, that is, an aid and furtherance of loyalty in my fellows."[5] Thurman's conception of loyalty, or as he usually referred to it, commitment, is very similar. Giving as examples the moral struggles of Paul and Lincoln as they struggled to find their highest loyalties, Thurman said loyalty was "the fusing of the outer and the inner ... The degree to which I yield myself to my participation [in a cause] is enlarged because my will becomes the will of the cause and the cause really forms my will and gives it back to me so that now it has staked out in me, itself."

At the very beginning I must acknowledge to you that along with countless other people in the English-speaking world who have thought seriously about the meaning of loyalty in any of its dimensions, I am deeply indebted to that great, winsome, sometimes devastating philosopher Josiah Royce, who during the early part of this century stated for the first time in definitive English the meaning of the philosophy of loyalty. Now I want to say that, because the ghost of Royce will be moving in and out of my mind as he has been for a long time. But I speak on my own authority.

What I want to do this morning is to lay what seems to me to be the fundamental foundation for a consideration for this very important and

---

of California in 1875. He studied in Europe and at Johns Hopkins, and in 1882 joined the faculty at Harvard, where he stayed for the remainder of his career, part of Harvard's "golden age of philosophy," with William James and George Santayana. Royce's philosophy had close affinities to the "absolute idealism" of Hegel and latter-day Hegelians. His students at Harvard included T. S. Eliot and W. E. B. Du Bois.

5. Royce, *Philosophy of Loyalty,* 118.

crucial experience of the human spirit. Everybody, despite the private and intensely personal and intimate life that he lives, everybody is involved in the social problem. I am not ever alone; I am never cut off from the social context, and therefore I must start as a human being with a body of material that is my heritage as a human being. And I become self-conscious only in relation to this social context. Now I want to take time to lay that down very carefully.

It is only when the little child becomes aware of the not-self that the child becomes aware of the self. I often wonder what is going on in a little baby's mind when his eyes begin to be eyes, when he begins to see, not just to expose his eyes, but when he begins to narrow the thing down. And he watches the object of his devotion, his mother, for instance, as she, after administering to his needs or cuddling him, puts him down. And then, he's watching all the time because he's not aware of her as over against himself. And then as he watches her she withdraws and his eyes follow. And there must be some moment of very great shock to the sensitive developing nervous system of the baby when the baby realizes that there is a not-self. There is that which is not really a part of him, but is close to him and is involved in all of his little feelings, but it isn't quite a part of him. And as he watches his mother separate herself from him it is then that his sense of isolation begins to emerge. And that sense of isolation takes a [word or phrase missing] in terms of separateness.

Now it is this fact that the individual becomes self-aware only initially in relation to that which is not the self but of which the self is conscious.

Now let's push this just a little. I become aware that I have a will of my own only when I am able to emerge with my will over against other wills. So it is true that I come to myself as a willing creature only as a result of my ability to differentiate my self from the social context in which I am living.

Now any self-conscious act on my part then must of necessity involve me directly and indirectly in the social heritage that has created me. Take the two passages that I read.[6] I'll get to loyalty. Just be patient. One, the Apostle Paul. "I didn't know," he said, "what covetousness was until the law said, 'Thou shalt not covet.'"[7] I was involved in the heritage, in all of the instruction, all that the law meant, I was in it. And it was I, and I was

---

6. The readings are not extant, but see footnotes 8 and 9 to this sermon.
7. Romans 7:7.

a creature of the law. But I was also a creature functioning in other relationships; and the law, because it was the dominant controlling, central fact of my world, it decided for me what would be my conscience, what would be a violation. The law says, "Thou shalt not," and when the law says, "Thou shalt not," then I say, "I shall not." So the law, because of its very nature, created for me whatever conscience that I have with reference to the way that I live my life. But deep within my relationship to the law I was a person, said Paul: I was conscious of impulses that rooted back in my biological past. There were great and unrestrained impulses that were a part of my nature that could not take into account the law. These impulses urging me to move in one direction and the law insisting that I move in another direction created in me a profound area of conflict, and I had to decide. And in honoring one, "the impulses of my body," as he calls it, I, says Paul, had to dishonor the other. So I split myself in two in an interesting kind of rationalization: With my mind I served the law of God while with my flesh I served the law of sin. And I can never find peace; I can never find happiness until I grasp willingly some transcending claim that will be for me so significant that in my relations to this claim my frustrations are resolved.

That's what he is saying. Who will deliver me from this body of death, this cleavage. Something, some dimension of synthesis that is capable of pulling together in the good old dialectic, the thesis and the antithesis. And he says God can do that. Therefore if I can respond as a self-conscious act to God then that will resolve my difficulty. That's the way he does with it.[8]

Abraham Lincoln: I want peace, peace for my land, my country. And as a commander in chief of all, the head man of the nation, it is my responsibility to be the living instrument of that kind of experience for my countrymen. I think that human slavery is evil. How can I work for peace if on this issue of human slavery we are divided? We have lived for more than one hundred years half-slave, half-free. But this dichotomy has

8. Thurman's description is of the difficult argument in Romans 7:7–25. A number of recent commentators argue that the passage is not autobiographical, as Thurman indicates, but is a more abstract discussion of Paul's continued need to find a rationale for his continued observance of Jewish law when all people can be saved from sin by sharing in the death and resurrection of Jesus. See "The Apostle Paul and the Introspective Conscience of the West," in Krister Stendahl, *Paul among Jews and Gentiles and Other Essays* (Philadelphia: Fortress Press, 1976), 78–96.

grown wider and wider and wider. The character of the divisiveness has become so devastating that at last we are involved in a great civil war. We cannot resolve it unless we can find some transcendent plane that pulls together the abolitionists and the slaveholders. And I've thought about it, said Lincoln, I've thought about it and I don't see the answer. For me the answer is the Union. And I have even said publicly that if in order to save the Union I must free half the slaves and hold the others, I will do that.[9] If in order to save the Union I must turn my back upon what seems to be to me the direct moral imperative that is implicit from any gross or refined understanding of the meaning of the democratic dogma, I'll do that. For the Union is the transcendent demand that is the creative synthesis capable of pulling together, resolving the thesis and the antithesis. But nobody wants to go along with me right now and I can't go on any longer. But what else am I going to do? "I can't go on and yet I must go on."[10]

Now, what is the meaning of all this? (And I'll be through pretty soon.) Loyalty seems to mean that there is a willing and thoroughgoing devotion of a person to a cause. Willing. Therefore, you see, loyalty can

---

9. This is a summary of Lincoln's letter (August 22, 1862) to newspaper publisher Horace Greeley: "I would save the Union . . . If I could save the Union without freeing *any* slave, I would do it; and if I could save it by freeing *all* the slaves, I would do it; and if I could save it by freeing some and leaving others alone, I would also do that"; see Abraham Lincoln, *Speeches and Writings, 1859–1865* (New York: Library of America, 1989), 357–58. Many Lincoln scholars have questioned whether this represented Lincoln's true views and point out that he had, as president-elect, rejected compromises that could have prevented Confederate secession but at the price of tying his hands about the future of slavery, and that the letter was an appeal to northern Democrats unconvinced of the need for abolition. By the time Lincoln wrote the letter, he was already determined to issue the Emancipation Proclamation, which he would do, in preliminary form, the following month.

10. Stephen Vincent Benét, *John Brown's Body* (Garden City, NY: Doubleday, Doran, 1928), 220. Benét's poem was a favorite of Thurman; see *PHWT*, 2: 78, 3: 249, and "The Green Bough" (February 12, 1961; in Folder 3, Box 12, HTC). In that sermon, Thurman argues that Lincoln resolved the dilemma of a nation divided between slavery and freedom by pushing himself to resolve to abolish slavery, whatever his constitutional cavils about the limits of his powers: "It is an amazing thing, what the logic of the commitment will lead a man to do, even though the thing that it finally leads him to do is something that he did not contemplate." In both sermons Thurman seems to be arguing Lincoln resolved his loyalties to the preservation of the Union and to his abhorrence of slavery but concluding that the Union could be preserved only by the abolition of slavery, and that a United States half free, half enslaved, could not be preserved.

never be acceptably realized if it makes a demand in which the will cannot concur. Willing. It is with reference to a cause, and here, I think, is what, for me at any rate, is a very important contribution that Josiah Royce makes to all the thinking that has been going on on this whole matter since 1906, in our country I mean. He insists that it is always with reference to a cause, to something that is in a sense outside of the individual, but to which the individual relates himself as a result of a self-conscious act of will. And therefore, you see, the demand of the cause becomes an inner response on the part of the individual. It is a willing and thoroughgoing devotion of the person to a cause.

Now of course you see, wherever that kind of response takes place, the individual becomes the living instance of the cause to which he is loyal. Now let's examine that principle just a little. Here we have our hands on something which is fundamental to the very structure of the universe, for what we are saying is that when the individual surrenders, yields his will to a cause, the cause then gives him back his will in order that that will may become the servant of the cause. You see?—don't know if I can make that clear—I give up my will in response to the cause, but the cause to which I am devoted then gives me back my will in order that I may put at the disposal of the cause all that I am.

Now you can do that to something that is not worthy of you. You can do that to something that isn't. Have you ever encountered anybody who fulfilled this requirement with reference to, oh let us say, having a certain kind of daisy in all the public parks in the United States? You know this is rather ridiculous. You've seen people who took just one little segment and it became their cause, that served the purpose of doing what? Of galvanizing all of the fragmentary aspects of their life into one whole. Galvanizing it into one unit so that this person now functions as a whole creature with reference to daisies. And wherever it happens, you see, there you will see a dynamic release of power, of energy, of vitality, even though the cause may not rate it at all. Because this is the kind of universe that is essentially dynamic in character, and whenever any individual places at the disposal of any single end and gives to that end his self-surrender, then there is released in that individual the limitless power of the universe so terrific in its character that it fuses all of the parts of the personality into a single whole. And that is why, instinctively, again and again, we resist the impact and the pull of anything that is capable of doing that for us. We don't want it because we live in little fragments, and every little fragment is precious and intimate and wonderful. And we don't want to give it up, so we reduce our exposure to anything that will inspire in us a whole-hearted response. We do that. That's what Augustine meant when he said, "Lord, make me a good man—but not yet."[11] Not yet.

Now just one more little step, if you just please. Loyalty then, and this is the basic insight for our morning, loyalty then is a word that we use to describe what is essentially a spiritual phenomenon derived from the nature of the universe. It means that it is the fusing of the outer and the inner. The cause to which I respond is external to me, and yet in some sense I participate in the cause, because I am a social creature. And the degree to which I yield myself to it, my participation is enlarged, because my will becomes the will of the cause, and the cause really forms my will and gives it back to me so that now it has staked out in me itself. Now what does that mean? Does it mean that I cannot be loyal to a person? Let's examine that for just a minute.

Loyalty to a person. What do we mean? I am loyal first, I am loyal to the tie that binds me to the person, and my loyalty to the person operates through the channel of the tie that relates me to the person. So in order to be true in this devotion to the tie, whatever tie it is, I will do no violence to the person. So my loyalty to the individual is a derivative, a secondary thing because the thing that is primary is my devotion to the tie that unites me and you—and you, and you, and you, and you.

Paul felt that he could be loyal to Paul only by being loyal to that which was capable of putting the parts of Paul together. Lincoln felt he could be loyal to Lincoln and to the slaves, to the Confederacy, to the Union and to himself only by being loyal to the tie, the transcendent tie that made of his relationships in all these dimensions one collective and synthesized whole. And that is what loyalty means. Are you loyal? Is there anything, any kind of cause or tie that relates you to your fellows?

---

11. Augustine, *Confessions* 8.7.

THE MEANING OF LOYALTY II

May 13, 1951
Fellowship Church

Thurman largely devotes his second sermon on loyalty to the problem of conflicting loyalties, those moments when an individual feels pulled in different directions by incompatible obligations. In 1937 he wrote, when making such a choice, "the ice is apt to be very thin." But complexity is not an excuse for inaction. When confronted with an either/or dilemma whose alternatives cannot be reconciled, one "must take sides."[1] In this sermon he writes that to make these decision, "the individual is always involved in relating himself to what may be regarded as a kind of hierarchy of causes." Thurman gives several examples. Following an argument he made in Jesus and the Disinherited, *he argues that "disadvantaged people" have "tended to survive by being true . . . to the experience, the raw experience of physical continuity" while denying their "loyalty to sincerity."[2] That is, those with less power try to survive by deceiving those with more power, and Thurman gives several examples, from songbirds playing dead to fool hawks to French resistance fighters evading Nazis.*

Thurman then discusses the conflict between loyalty to "genuineness and sincerity" and "loyalty to mercy," when one deceives, not out of fear but from a desire to not needlessly hurt another person. Finally, Thurman looks at instances when "loyalty to my faith which becomes the creative manifestation of the total meaning of loyalty to me, if my faith means really my faith," using the biblical example of Naaman the leper. The challenge for Naaman,

---

1. HT, "The Significance of Jesus VI: [untitled]" (September 1937), in *PHWT,* 2: 87–88. For other references to conflicts of loyalties, see *PHWT,* 2: 109, 343.

2. HT, *Jesus and the Disinherited* (New York: Abingdon-Cokesbury, 1949), 58–73.

and those in similar situations, was to separate true faith from social obligations to external religious observances.

For Thurman, conflicts between loyalties can force an individual away from the easy, the comfortable, and the socially acceptable, and toward a more challenging understanding of the meaning of their life. In another sermon in this series, not included here, Thurman sees Job as perhaps the epitome of a person of conflicting loyalties, the standoff "when the logic of the mind says 'Yes,' and the logic of the heart says 'No.'" Thurman's Job thinks that "my heart says that God can't be evil. My heart says keep on worshiping God even though worshiping God in the midst of what you are going through your mind tells you that you are a fool. How shall I cast my vote?"[3] When confronted with such a deadlock, you can only decide with the entirety of your life, making the choice, as Thurman titled his autobiography, "with head and heart."

It was suggested last Sunday that loyalty is defined as the willing and steadfast and practical devotion of a person to a cause. And further, that the basis of loyalty, the heart of loyalty, is what [Josiah] Royce calls loyalty to loyalty, which becomes for him the basis for all morality and ethics.

Now I want to pick up the thread from last Sunday and deal today, and if I don't get through, next Sunday morning, with the meaning of loyalty as it has bearing on the problems that arise from conflict between loyalties. And I would like for you to be as open-minded and as uninhibited as possible so that, as we work along together and you hear me say something with which you cannot possibly be in agreement, when that moment happens you will have the kind of discipline and self-control that will permit your mind to remain open for the rest of our working together and then you can close it this afternoon.

Life would be very simple if it would be reduced to a single solitary objective cause and that personality were so simple that it could in all of its aspects relate itself to a single objective cause. But because of the very complexity of personality and because of the very complexity of the

---

3. HT, "The Meaning of Loyalty IV: Job's Dilemma" (May 17, 1951), HTC.

involvement of living experiences we are called upon again and again to exercise selectivity in causes to which we shall relate ourselves. It is for this reason, I think, that Dr. Royce tries to cut through all the hierarchy of causes as such and insists that loyalty in its essence is loyalty to loyalty—*loyalty to loyalty*. That I am regarding every cause as a vehicle that provides a hook, as it were, upon which I may hang my loyalty.

Now it is obvious that conflicts arise between loyalties because at any particular moment I may be related to a cause, to a purpose, to an end, which cause or purpose or end is paramount at the moment, is most significant at the moment, but in the light of the total context of my life it may not be the most significant purpose or cause for me. I want to break this down in simple and comprehensible categories. Let us look at two or three.

[Consider] the conflict that arises when I am faced with the loyalty to the recognized and willingly embraced and accepted ideal of sincerity, for instance, and the loyalty to the continuous physical existence of my own life on the other hand. Shall I be true in terms of genuineness and sincerity, loyal to that even, if it means the destruction or the annihilation of my own life?

Now as we sit here in the quietness of this room that question may be academic. But it is one of the oldest moral and ethical problems and struggles of the life of man. In any kind of society, in any period of human history where there have been weak and disadvantaged people living side by side with strong and advantaged people, the weak people have tended to survive by being true to this insistence upon loyalties to the raw experience of physical continuity, even as at moments they have denied the validity of the claim of loyalty to sincerity. Curious isn't it. The weak kept alive by fooling the strong. And we don't think anything about it when we see the thing operating in nature. I have mentioned to you perhaps several times, but when I was a boy in Florida I spent much of my time in the summer in the woods. And one of the things that always impressed me was the uncanny way in which birds (I know them when I see them but I don't know their names, but they were birds) could tell from the outline of the shadow of the hawk that the hawk was about. And then they would literally play dead. Literally fall over and sometimes with a little grass in their toes. The hawk perhaps blinked his eyes and went on about his business thinking he had had an optical illusion, hoping he would come upon a meadow in which there were little birds that didn't have sense enough to play dead.

Now when we see that operating in the world of nature it doesn't present for us a problem of moral and ethical consequence. When we turn to the book of Ezekiel and we read the consolation and the words of comfort and assurance that the prophet was giving to the Judaites in exile in Babylon, and as we read those words and read them very carefully and we see that he is using a term like Hiram of Tyre[4]—but the description of Hiram of Tyre is recognized by scholars as the description of Nebuchadnezzar. But Ezekiel could not say to the Judaites in Babylon, well I'm talking about Nebuchadnezzar. So he put the whole thing on poor old Hiram of Tyre, and every Judaite who listened to him recognized what he was doing, but the Babylonian secret service couldn't do anything with it because he wasn't talking about Babylon, he was talking about Hiram.

When the underground in France and parts of Europe during the days of the German domination, when they were deceptive, when they used every subterfuge to keep the enemy from recognizing who they were and what they were doing, did we have any moral judgment about that? In the conflict between loyalties—to loyalty to the ideal of freedom, or loyalty to the ideal of self-preservation, over against loyalty to the ideal of genuineness and sincerity as touching the tyrants?

Can I be loyal to loyalty and thereby increase the total sum of loyalty without honoring the loyalty of a man who is loyal to a cause, which, in my judgment, is an evil cause? What about it? Or is it possible for me to honor his loyalty in order that my loyalty might increase the sum total of loyalty in the human experience and at the same time, as a result of my loyalty, I must seek to destroy the cause to which he is loyal?

Or let us look at another aspect of this. The loyalty to the ideal of genuineness and sincerity as it may be brought into sharp conflict with the loyalty to mercy. You may not want to think about this. But it's all right. Henry Van Dyke wrote the rather famous Christmas tale *The Story of the Other Wise Man,* and in one of the passages the other wise man

---

4. Ezekiel does not mention Hiram of Tyre, a Phoenician king who flourished several centuries earlier, but only the "prince of Tyre (Ezekiel 28:2). This reference to the Phoenicians is mysterious. Thurman's is only one of several interpretations.

walked into a courtyard where he finds a cottage and in that cottage there is a Jewish matron with her little two-year-old baby boy. She's hiding in the corner because as she hears the footsteps of the other wise man she thinks that he is part of Herod's army coming to carry out his command to kill all male boys under two years old. And as soon as the other wise man comes in and sees her in this fear-stricken condition, he hears the footsteps and the rhythmic beat of Herod's soldiers as they come into the courtyard. And he walks to the open door to meet the captain of Herod's hosts. And Herod's captain says, "Is there a male child in this house?" And the other wise man says, "No! There is no male child in this house. But here is a ruby." And the captain has sense enough to go on down the street. And when Van Dyke wrote *The Other Wise Man*, he was a senior chaplain of all the armed forces of the United States; greatly beloved, a Christian poet and a certain kind of philosopher and preacher. And there was just a tidal wave of protest because it seemed as if he was putting a premium upon lying.[5]

The most searching experience . . . and you will pardon the very personal reference here. Perhaps after I tell you this you will decide that, well, you may decide anything you care to. But the first year that I was out of Divinity School and was studying in Oberlin, I had a little church in the community. And one day I received a telephone call from Steuben, Ohio, saying that the wife of one of the officers of our little church had been seriously injured in an automobile accident and she had asked for me and would I please come over at once. A friend of mine who had an automobile drove me over to Steubenville. We found the little hospital and we went to it. I identified myself to the nurse on the ward and the nurse said, "It was a very serious accident. Her brother was killed instantly when the car turned over. We don't think she can live. Please go in but don't stay longer than two or three minutes. You must not do anything to shock her, but give her comfort if you can."

---

5. Henry Van Dyke, *The Story of the Other Wise Man* (New York: Harper & Brothers, 1896). Van Dyke (1855–1933) was a Presbyterian minister who taught English literature at Princeton University from 1899 to 1923, and was a prolific author on religion and other subjects, and was moderately liberal in his theological views. In 1913 his former Princeton colleague Woodrow Wilson appointed him ambassador to the Netherlands, and he remained in that post until 1916. After the American entrance into World War I, he became a naval chaplain.

She was all bandaged and terribly broken as to body and limb. I could only hear what she said by holding my ears very close to her lips just to pick up the muted whisper between her agonies. And she said, "Please read the 17th chapter of John."[6] Well, I quoted all the 17th chapter of John that I knew. And then she said, "Will you pray with me?" And I said, "I am doing that." And then there was silence and then she said, "Is my brother dead?" And I said, "No, he isn't dead." Then I left. Well, I didn't sleep much that night. Finally Sunday came, and before I could preach my sermon to my congregation I told them what I had done. I said I had to decide in a split minute what I would do, and I did the thing which at that time seemed to me to be right. The thing that disturbed me now, and that argued against it all, was that perhaps she would not live, and the last thing that she asked of her minister, he deceived her. And I said to them I don't know what kind of judgment you will have of me for it, and perhaps you will not even want me to remain as your minister. But to me, in that instant I chose to be loyal to mercy. I do not offer it as a general principle, but in that incident that is the way I behaved, and perhaps if I faced another thing of that sort I might not. I don't know.

Well, she lived, and the first time I went to see her when she was back home—we didn't talk about this when I would go to see her in the hospital, nothing was ever said—but when I went to see her when she came back home, she said, "I notice that you have never said anything to me about your first visit to the hospital." And I said, "No, I haven't." She said, "I knew my brother was dead, but I am so glad you made it as easy for me as you could." Well that made me feel better.

What do you do? It's not an academic question. What do you do? The loyalty to loyalty, which means that in your loyalty you shall add to the sum total of the loyalty experiences of the race, demands of you that in the presence of loyalty to mercy, if you are sure that that is what it is, and your loyalty to genuineness stands over against the loyalty to mercy, how do you cast your votes? What would you do? As you think about what I did, what would you do? What would inform the quality of your religious insight at that point?

---

6. John 17 consists of a long prayer by Jesus to God the Father.

Loyalty to loyalty. Is there a cause for which the answer is to be loyal to the experience of loyalty itself? [One] that provides the principle that can be introduced in any situation however complex and complicated the situation may be, and result totally in the increase, in the confidence, that the human spirit has in the integrity of personality? What about it? Let me illustrate. It's much better to talk in terms of windows. Let's take just one more step, loyalty, loyalty to my faith which becomes the creative manifestation of the total meaning of loyalty to me, if my faith means really my faith. When I am face to face with the behavior that might attack the integrity of another man's faith—Let me illustrate. It's much better to talk in terms of windows.[7]

There was a man whose name was Naaman in 2 Kings, a very great leader, a prime minister and commander in chief of the armies of King Aram.[8] He was a wonderful man but he had leprosy. It happened that when his armies had overrun a certain area they had taken captive a little Jewish girl. And this little Jewish girl became the maidservant of the king's wife. And when she heard that this man, Naaman, had leprosy, she said to the king's wife, "I just wish that he would go over to Samaria, and let the prophet[9] there cure him because the prophet can cure him." And the word went from that little private women's quarters to the king, and then the king passed the word on to Naaman and so they set forth. He had a lot of gifts and things he was going to carry, and he went over to Samaria and found the prophet and sent word to the prophet that he believed that he could heal him. And the prophet didn't even come out to look at him. The prophet just said, you go and bathe in the water[10] seven times. And Naaman was incensed! He said, "He did not even have com-

---

7. "Window" is a term Thurman often used to refer to an additional portion of a sermon, a way of seeing something new, a portal to insight and knowledge. See also p. 112.

8. The story of Naaman and King Aram is told in 2 Kings 5. It is a story Thurman appreciated for its universalist implications and its caution against self-righteous fanaticism. Loyalty, even to one's highest and most fervently held truths, at times must be tempered with mercy. Thurman often told the story of Naaman the leper; see "Introduction: Man and the Moral Struggle," in HT, *Moral Struggle and the Prophets*, 6–7; *PHWT*, 4: 27–28.

9. The prophet Elisha.

10. The river Jordan.

mon courtesy enough to come out and talk to me face to face but sent some underling to me to tell me to go and bathe. I'm not dirty." But somebody else in the group said, "Well it isn't much to ask to do. You have leprosy, and you don't have any choice if you want to just try—you can't lose anything because you have it." So he went and dipped himself in the water, and he came out clean, and as the chronicler says, he came out with the skin of a baby.

So he wanted to give gifts to the prophet, but the prophet said, "No, I don't want anything." But he said, "Let me take two mule wagons full of soil." You see at that time God or Jehovah was a national God, and he had no power if he were operating in a foreign land, you see. So unless there was some soil that he would feel at home in . . . there is a sort of nationalism that is in the background of our whole faith at this point. So he said, "There is just one other request that I want to make: When in carrying out my duties of state, and the king, leaning on my arm, walks into the Temple of Rimmon,[11] and when he genuflects at the altar of the Temple of Rimmon, and I as his support genuflect also, will the Eternal forgive me if I behave in accordance with the demands of my office even though those demands are in violation of my commitment to the Eternal?" It's a tremendous problem. "My heart is not in the bowing. The altar of Rimmon means nothing to me, but it is the center of the worship and devotion of my king and he leans upon me. Shall I do violence to the sanctity of his religious experience in order that I might be true?" . . . [*The extant version of the sermon ends here, before its conclusion.*]

---

11. Rimmon is a Syrian god.

The Meaning of Loyalty III:
The State

May 20, 1951
Fellowship Church

In the third of the sermons on loyalty, Thurman first discusses how an individual can find their highest loyalties through "the willing and steadfast and practical devotion of a person to a cause." Throughout his career, this discernment was perhaps the key moment of religious self-discovery.[1] As he writes here, these decisions are involving "at every level of his other causes and at every level of his other commitments . . . It follows that the degree to which an individual is true to that, is loyal to that, to that degree does he contribute to the sum total of loyalty of his fellows; and to that degree does his loyalty become contagious in its radical effect upon the individuals who themselves are trying to be loyal to an ultimate cause, an ultimate goal. It is the moment beyond all other moments that the true basis of human worth is established."

Much of the rest of the sermon is concerned with the potential conflict between such ultimate loyalties and loyalty to the state, in an oblique but unmistakable reference to the recent controversy in California about "loyalty oaths" for state employees. There is a legitimate role for nationalism, when it functions as "the feeling of sharing in the same body of hope and collective experiences; it is a sense of participation in one dream, in one destiny." But when a narrow nationalist ideology becomes an official state doctrine and requires that the "individual in the state relates . . . to some organizational structure, some party, some individuals, some office; and to that

---

1. For Thurman on personal self-discovery as an essential religious act, see "Finding God," in *PHWT*, 1: 110–15; and "The Sources of Power for Christian Action," and "Christian, Who Calls Me Christian?," in *PHWT*, 2: 93–100; 106–13.

*degree does the state move into the centrality of the position which, in my
definition of loyalty, you see, only God should occupy." Can the conflicting
loyalties of nationality and individual conscience be reconciled? He pointed
to the example of Gandhi, who tried to ensure that "the political expression
of the will to live, the organized and collective agreement upon which men
lived in a stable society, that that would be vehicular for expressing the true
loyalty of the human spirit which is the loyalty to truth—to me, to God—
which is the ultimate basis of self-respect." As with Gandhi, the American
civil rights movement would face similar challenges in reconciling the paramount centrality of individual conscience and ultimate loyalties with the
needs of a mass movement and the need for state action and intervention.*

We have been thinking together for several Sunday mornings now
about the meaning of loyalty in the experience of man. And last
Sunday we talked about various levels of conflict between loyalties. Today
I want to take the discussion last Sunday just another step. And I hope
that I will soon be through with this discussion.

Loyalty as defined in our working hypothesis here: the willing and
steadfast and practical devotion of a person to a cause. There is a hierarchy
of causes, of course, and the conflict arises often because of the conflict in
the relative significance of the causes to which one is dedicated.

Now this morning I want to take the development that loyalty finally
rests upon the devotion of the individual: the willing, the self-conscious,
and deliberate devotion of the individual to a cause which to him is
supremely worthful. Takes us another step, you see. And in relation to its
supreme worth and significance, the ultimate basis of self-respect for the
individual is established and guaranteed. In the light of the commitment,
the devotion to what is to the individual a supremely worthful cause,
that commitment becomes at once the basis for the individual's ethics;
it becomes at once the basis of the individual's values; it becomes at once
the definition of the terms upon which the individual will live his life. It
involves him, therefore, at every level of his other causes and at every level
of his other commitments. It is an ultimate devotion.

And it follows that the degree to which an individual is true to that,
is loyal to that, to that degree does he contribute to the sum total of loy-

alty of his fellows; and to that degree does his loyalty become contagious in its radical effect upon the individuals who themselves are trying to be loyal to an ultimate cause, an ultimate goal. It is that moment beyond all other moments that the true basis of human worth is established. It is the awareness on the part of the individual that he has apprehended that which is of ultimate significance and worthfulness. And of course, we need not be disturbed or our minds disarranged because of the different labels by which this is named. To me the ultimate cause that has the final definitive, searching, penetrating, invasive demand of the human spirit is God. You may say truth; you may say the supreme good. I don't care. That is not my affair. But to me it is God.

And by that I mean that there does come a time when I am face to face with an ultimate scrutiny; when I am without any pretense; when I am no longer involved in the estimate of my fellows, where all of the arrangements that have given to my life relative measures of stability and significance seem to be without merit and without significance; when I am stripped; when I am driven back upon the literal substance of my very self; when I, the human spirit, am brought face to face with God, the adversary. It is the idea that is expressed in Job. "I've wrestled with tragedy; I've wrestled with loss of family, of disease, with the loss of status, with the loss of a certain kind of character. But none of those things measure me. I must find out what is my true genius; what is my true worth." So Job says, "Behold I go forward, and he isn't there; backwards, I cannot perceive him. Where is he? Let me track him down through all the universe or let him track me down until at last there is nothing between me and him. And in that moment of scrutiny, what I am, in its true character, will remain."[2] Now that's the ultimate basis for loyalty.

Now any other cause, you see, becomes a secondary cause, which is interesting. So let's pursue it now. Any other cause becomes a secondary cause. And the significance of causes is defined for the person in terms of the degree to which a particular cause seems to be vehicular for making available to the spirit the transcendent quality of that kind of experience. Now this is the true basis of the conflict of loyalty between man and the state. This is it! This is it!

---

2. Thurman is paraphrasing Job, the subject of his next week's sermon; see HT, "The Meaning of Loyalty IV: Job's Dilemma" (May 17, 1951), HTC.

Loyalty to country. Let's talk about that for a little. There is a fundamental distinction, in my judgment, between the—let's see now; I want to say this right—between the genius of any particular nationalism, for instance, and the state. Nationalism must always have a local center. It is the fundamental experience of individuals in the midst of neighbors; in the midst of the overarching understanding and benediction of a common dialect, or language; it is the feeling of sharing in the same body of hope and collective experiences; it is a sense of participation in one dream, in one destiny. All of that is the genius of nationalism. It has to do with the humanizing process in which the human animal moves collectively and with some measure of creativity. Now the state is, in a sense you see, the vehicle, the expression, the formal expression of this collective, psychological, and from my point of view social and spiritual experience of the people.

Now the degree to which the state becomes the agent of that, to that degree does the state become an instrument in the hands of the fulfillment of the genius of that kind of collective stirring and collective experience on a segment of the human family. And when the state becomes that, then it also becomes involved in making and sensitizing itself to that same kind of process that may be going on in some other part of the world. And any attack upon that process in any part of the world becomes an act of violence upon the process as it is going on in this part of the world. All right. And therefore, the individuals who are involved in that have a cause, and the cause emerges out of their collective experiences, you see? And the degree to which that cause becomes vehicular—the degree to which that cause does not conflict, does not do violence to this initial thing about which I was talking at the very beginning—to that degree there is no conflict between patriotism on the one hand and great religious devotion on the other.

But now, when the state becomes an instrumentality divorced from this ground and becomes an end in itself and insists that the individual in the state relates himself not to this movement but to some organizational structure, some party, some individuals, some office, to that degree does the state move into the centrality of the position which, in my definition of loyalty, you see, only God should occupy.

Now a dictator always recognizes that, they are very smart people, because one of the first things that he insists upon doing is this. He must become—how should I say it?—the kind of ambulating epitome of the state itself so that he is not "X" with a name who was born in a certain way, who eats and gets hungry and weeps and who has a temper, but he is the state! And any loyalty that demands of any member of the body politic that that member of the body politic shall put anything in competition with the centrality of the state becomes at once, you see, a threat to the very security upon which the dictator rests; upon which that kind of national state rests.

Now it follows then, you see, that one of the first moves that must be made is the cutting off of any relatedness on the part of the individual in such a state to any cause, whether that is to God or anything else that may be competitive to the central cause, the central loyalty. Then the whole concept of religious experience and religious orientation must be re-thought so that God and the state, or God and the dictator, may become one and the same. And any idea that is in competition with that has to be destroyed. Any individual who participates in that or recognizes an orientation that transcends the loyalty to the state or the dictator has to be liquidated.

Now I'm interested in applying this, and I am sorry the time is running out, but in practical terms this means that as long as an individual can be rooted and easily committed to the kind of nationalism about which I have been thinking, and make that nationalism vehicular or expressive of this major, dominant loyalty which ultimately gives to the individual the basis of her own self-estimate and self-respect, there is no conflict, in my judgment, between that kind of patriotism and a recognition of a transcendent cause. But it is contingent, you see, upon the willing, the self-conscious yielding of the devotion and personality. And that is why I can understand and appreciate the provisions that are made in our constitution for loyalty to the country, to the state. That seems to me to have a very creative logic in it that is fundamental to the very genius of the experience of group belonging. It is inherent in the whole process of sharing the common life. I can understand that. But I cannot understand at all in terms of the meaning either of loyalty or of religious experience anything beyond that formal insistence that men declare themselves in terms of the registering of their ultimate loyalty, non-competitive loyalty to a state. That I cannot understand.

Now there is one more step I want to take. There is something very instructive in the life—that much overworked life—of Mahatma Gandhi on this whole issue. Mr. Gandhi by his own definition recognized a transcendent loyalty to what he called truth. The truth became the ultimate basis of his self-respect. And where he uses the term "truth," I for my own orientation and background use the term "God."[3] And he felt that any relationship, any tool, any instrumentality that men might use to unscramble themselves from any particular predicament, however terrible that predicament is, even the tool itself must be vehicular to truth, which is the transcendent loyalty. So when he decided to break the law and march against—to break the salt business—and to march down to the sea, he informed the British government that he was going to do that: the time and place so they could take whatever measures were necessary.[4] Because he felt subversive about it, to be secretive about it would be an utter violation of the spirit of truth to which he felt that men owed their transcendent loyalty. And the rival political machinery they used in an effort to work out a whole series of secondary loyalties, that machinery itself must be instrumental or be vehicular for and to the basic loyalty to truth which is the ground, the ultimate ground, for the self respect of the individual human spirit.[5]

And so when I asked him, "Why did your technique of non-violence fail in its objective?"—namely, to bring freedom to the Indian people, and he said, "It failed because a great creative spiritual ideal like that which has its root in man's relationship to truth could not be sustained over a time interval of sufficient duration to be effective, because there wasn't enough vitality in the people to sustain it. They began after a while introducing elements in the method that denied the integrity of man's relation to truth." They became violent, he said. Bitterness arose, hatred arose.

---

3. Gandhi's term for nonviolent action or truth force was *satyagraha*. Gandhi's autobiography was titled *The Story of My Experiments with Truth,* originally published in 1929.

4. Gandhi led his march to the sea to protest the British salt law in March–April 1930.

5. Thurman, for the remainder of his sermon, reviews his 1936 conversation with Gandhi. See "With Our Negro Guests," in *PHWT,* 1: 332–39.

But, he said, I felt that if they had enough vitality they could do it. So I quit what I was doing and began working on the problem of vitality, for I felt that that is where the secret is. Not changing my method; not trying to find a method that was less congenial to the spirit of truth but more practical in terms of the short-range experience of the Indian people for their freedom. Which is always the temptation, you see. So the first thing I did was to analyze it. And I analyzed it, and I found that they lacked vitality for two reasons. One reason was that they were hungry. Eighty-five, ninety million of them lived from childhood until the time of their death without ever once having the experience of a full stomach. In the normal times that is true and they lacked vitality, and I felt that if somehow I could find, I could reactivate an age-old technique which they had used, namely, the spinning wheel, and make that spinning wheel vehicular in terms of this over-mastering, basic loyalty; then the spinning wheel in turn in its practical aspect would begin to build within them some tissue growing out of the reestablishing of a new kind of economic pattern for their existence.

And the second thing: the basis of their lack of self-respect was the presence of untouchability in Hinduism. Here were eighty-five or ninety-five million people who were outside the very pale; outside of any sense of ethical and moral and spiritual responsibility. They had no grounds for human dignity; they could not experience even deep within them-selves any basis for ultimate self-respect because they were denied the very genius of truth itself by withholding from them all what the root of their religion, Hinduism, meant to them.

And therefore, he said, I decided to change their names from outcaste or pariahs or Shudras[6] to Harijans, which means "child of God."[7] I felt that if I could make all caste Hindus call all outcaste Hindus "children of God" then the constant repetition of that would create within them the kind of moral block that could not be relieved as it built and built and

6. Shudras are the lowest of the four Indian castes in the classic taxonomy, but higher than the outcastes.

7. Gandhi opposed untouchability but not the caste system as such, and insisted, in the 1935 British Indian census, that they be counted as Hindus rather than in their own group, as their most prominent leaders preferred. Dalit, not Harijan, became the most popular term for outcastes, as Gandhi's term was widely seen as patronizing.

built until they changed their social attitude toward them. So I worked at it on that basis, all the time trying to do what? Trying to make, to guarantee that the political expression of the will to live, the organized and collective agreement upon which men lived in a stable society, that that would be vehicular for expressing the true loyalty of the human spirit which is the loyalty to truth—to me, to God—which is the ultimate basis of self-respect.

THE DECLARATION OF INDEPENDENCE I: CREATED EQUAL

July 29, 1951
Fellowship Church

Shortly after completing his sermon series on "The Meaning of Loyalty" in June 1951, Thurman embarked on another sermon series with a political theme, four sermons on the Declaration of Independence. Although he pays some attention to its historical context, especially in this initial sermon, that is not their main purpose. Thurman in these essays emphasizes the promise of the Declaration, especially the four key terms of its preamble, equality, life, liberty, and the pursuit of happiness. He makes clear his disagreements with Thomas Jefferson's understanding of some of the key terms of the Declaration, and mentions, though does not discuss at length, Jefferson's fraught connections with the institution of slavery.

In this sermon, on equality, he defends his belief that the only true measure of equality is the "equality of infinite worth" possessed by every person.[1] For Thurman this is an existential equality: "My life is rooted in a kind of awareness of my meaning that does not arise from your interpretation of my significance, [and] that no judgment that you impose upon me, no order of society into which you seek to have me regimented, can sever my roots

---

1. Thurman borrowed the idea of the "equality of infinite worth" from Henry A. Myers, *Are Men Equal? An Inquiry into the Meaning of American Democracy* (New York: Putnam, 1945); see HT, "To Henry A. Myers" (May 28, 1945), in *PHWT*, 3: 130–31. Myers argued that "the idea of equality has its source in the private man's sense of his own infinite worth" for "all immortal souls are equally precious in the eyes of God" (Myers, *Are Men Equal?*, 160, 161). Thurman's first use of the term is probably in "The Fascist Masquerade" (1946) in *PHWT*, 3: 158. More broadly, Thurman's notion of the infinite worth of the individual is probably derived from his study of the German mystic Meister Eckhart; see HT, *The Way of the Mystics*, 82–90.

from the dimension of awareness that gives to me my inner significance."
This transcends political equality, but is, for Thurman, the necessary basis
of any just society, such as the one incompletely outlined in the Declaration
of Independence.

[This is][2] the first in a series of sermons on the religious foundation or basis of the Declaration of Independence.[3] We have been thinking together for weeks now about the meaning of religion, and particularly the religion of Jesus to the disinherited peoples of the earth, and one of the insights that has come from our thinking together, our hope, is that the insights of religion, if they be valid for the disinherited, the same insights must be valid[4] for all other peoples, which is another way of suggesting through a rather laborious series of thinkings together that the truths of religion are true because they are universally true and not because they appear merely in religion.[5]

As a background for our thinking this morning, I want to read a little from the Book of Micah: "But in the last days it shall come to pass that the mountain of the [gap in recording][6] ... [In 1790, when George Washington assumed office][7] he answered the letter written to him upon his inauguration as the first president of the United States by a small

---

2. Hypothetical reconstruction of missing opening.

3. There are four extent sermons in the Declaration of Independence sermon series, all printed in the current volume.

4. In the recording of the sermon, Thurman apparently stated that "the insights of religion, if they be valid for the disinherited, the same insights must be invalid for all other peoples." The editors think it likely that Thurman misspoke when he said the "same insights must be invalid," but the sentence can be construed in a number of alternative ways.

5. A dilemma that was first posed in Plato's dialogue *Euthyphro* (ca. 399–395 BCE). Thurman often argued, as here, that the truths of religion are universally true.

6. The recording was cut off when Thurman recited the passage from the fourth chapter of Micah. We do not know how much of the chapter he read, but presumably he at least read through Micah 4:4: "And they shall dwell each man beneath his vine and beneath his fig tree." The first verses are essentially identical to Isaiah 2:2–4. Thurman is arguing that the spiritual universality of the Hebrew prophets and the emphasis on the common creation of all humanity in God's image were duplicated in the vision of the authors of the Declaration of Independence.

7. Opening of sentence is missing; this is a conjectural reconstruction.

community of Jewish people who wanted him to know how deeply committed they were out of the vast historical experience of their lives to the ideals for which this country stood, and in his reply he said to them that he hoped that the time would never come when it would not be possible for every man to worship under his own vine and fig tree and no man need be afraid.[8]

We hold these truths to be self-evident, that all men are created equal. That is as far as we will go this morning. I mean, I'm not sitting down . . . I don't mean that [laughter]. That's good. All men are created equal.

We want to deal with the question of equality. When we look at objects in nature or deal with time, we give to it a certain character, a character which these objects do not have: color, warmth, or coldness are qualities which we, the observer, give to these various objects.[9] So, [John Locke] says these qualities are the result of their impact upon us and our reaction to them. Now, the meaning of that in terms of our problem is that what we call the mental substance, which is a part of the characteristic of mind, the thing that makes me give these things a certain quality, is independent of the object of nature. It is, in a sense, private and personal and unique and it cannot be invaded by anything outside.

Now every human being has that characteristic in common. Every human being starts out then, he goes on, as a kind of blank sheet[10] on which is written, as he grows and develops, the impressions of all the

8. President George Washington responded to the Hebrew Congregation in Newport, Rhode Island, on August 18, 1790, thanking them for an earlier letter of support, writing, "may the Children of the Stock of Abraham, who dwell in this land, continue to merit and enjoy the good will of the other Inhabitants; while every one shall sit in safety under his own vine and fig tree, and there shall be none to make him afraid" (George Washington, *Writings* [New York: Library of America, 1997], 767). At the time, the United States was the only country that gave Jews the rights of full citizenship. The Constitution abolished religious tests for holding federal office. The congregation's home, the Touro synagogue, built in 1763, is the oldest standing Jewish house of worship in the United States.

9. Without explicitly identifying him, Thurman is discussing the epistemology of the English philosopher John Locke (1632–1704), who argued in *An Essay Concerning Human Understanding* (1689) for the distinction between primary qualities of objects, such as shape and solidity, that exist independent of observers, and secondary qualities, such as color and taste, which do not.

10. This is Locke's notion of the mind at birth as a blank sheet, or *tabula rasa*, which is imprinted and shaped by external sensations.

things around him. Now when Thomas Jefferson,[11] who was the sire of the Declaration of Independence, as far as writing it down is concerned and perhaps as far as getting the ideas pooled, when he says that we hold these truths to be self-evident, he is appealing to man's general experience with nature and the world and with each other, a general assumption that it is obvious that men are equal in their relationships to the world of nature, etc.[12] Then he isn't content to deal with or to rest his case on the fact that these truths are self-evident, but he has to make an appeal to something more than that, which is obvious to the rational mind. He says: We hold these truths to be self-evident that all men are *created* equal. That is an appeal to the dogma, that's an appeal to the Bible, that is an appeal to the historic religion of the culture and the civilization. And the root of the notion that men are created equal and therefore are equal is to be found primarily in the profound and significant insights of the prophets of Israel, and it is their contribution through the channel of religion as it emerges in Western civilization that makes the case for the fact that men are created equal. How do they do it? The prophet Ezekiel, for instance—remember how we were talking about him when we were discussing the whole question of loyalty?[13] The prophet Ezekiel insisted that the group is not responsible merely for the individual, but that the individual was responsible himself. I cannot say that my group is responsible for what I do. The prophet Ezekiel insisted that every man is responsible for his own behavior, that the ultimate fact about human experience is the fact of personal responsibility for what one does. And it's amazing how hundreds, thousands of years later, that notion appears

---

11. Thomas Jefferson (1743–1826), the primary author of the Declaration of Independence, and the third president of the United States.

12. Thurman is arguing that Lockean epistemology as well as Locke's political thought guided Thomas Jefferson in drafting the Declaration of Independence; that is, because our minds start life without an innate structure of ideas, we all start from an initial position of equality, we all have to learn from experience and nature, and in this regard we are equal. The further implication for Thurman is that every person has an equal mental freedom to shape their own lives as they choose, whatever their external physical or political constraints.

13. Thurman discussed Ezekiel two months earlier in "The Meaning of Loyalty II," printed in the current volume. The following year he would deliver a sermon on Ezekiel, "The Meaning of Ezekiel," printed in HT, *Moral Struggle and the Prophets* (Maryknoll, NY: Orbis Books, 2020), 175–87.

in contemporary psychology, primarily in Adlerian psychology, that the individual is responsible for his own actions, that one of the problems of modern life is to insist that the individual be responsible for his own actions, rather than that their cousin should be responsible, or that their father was responsible, or their mother should be responsible.[14]

This takes a very simple form in the development of Israel in a thing called the temple tax. I call your attention to it because I think that we cannot believe deeply or function effectively on behalf of the democratic ideal if somehow the structure of the thing is not grasped and understood by the mind. So the Israelites felt that the temple tax provided the one radical and simple illustration of the fact that all, all of the Israelites, were created equal. The temple tax was a small amount that every Jew, everywhere, had to pay, whether he lived in Palestine and was a part of the temple worship or whether he was scattered to the ends of the earth, and the amount was the same. And there was a movement on the part of some of the more well-to-do people who felt that, "Why should we not just give an endowment and let the endowment keep alive the public worship of God?" And it was the Pharisees who insisted that that could not be true because if a small group of people guaranteed the public worship of God, then that meant that the average limited individual who was only able to give just a little bit would be cut off from participation in the formal act of public worship, so that they maintained that the temple tax that everybody had to pay, wherever he was, must be small enough to be within reach of everybody, which meant that each person paid a symbolic tribute to the fact that in the presence of God, he was as good as any other man or equal to any other man.

Now, when Thomas Jefferson was working, trying to get this Declaration developed, get it accepted, he wanted to put into the Declaration of Independence that slavery was something that the colonies were not responsible for, something that the British had brought with them, and

---

14. Alfred Adler (1870–1937) was an Austrian psychologist and psychoanalyst, originally associated with Freud, but later he founded his own school of Individual Psychology, probably best known for popularizing the idea of the "inferiority complex." He moved to the United States with the rise of Hitler.

there was a very stormy argument about it.[15] And the argument resulted in the fact that it doesn't appear; no reference to slavery appears in the Declaration because the feeling, the political feeling was: we are having a hard enough time to make our case for independence from Britain, now if we drag into that the whole question of slavery, then it means that we will never get free, which was a fairly interesting observation.[16]

We hold these truths to be self-evident, that all men are created equal. Created equal. Do you believe that? I don't want to hurry through this. I want you to think, just feel along. Equality as to what? All men do not have the same talents. All men do not have the same gifts. It is very interesting that the philosopher felt that all men were created equal as to capacity, and at the same time he recognized the fact that men varied in their abilities to do this or that or the other. But you see, with the notion that the body is a material substance in which the mental substance is resident, then if there is any limitation placed on the expression of the mental substance the limitation is not in the quality of the mental substance but is in the material substance, the body, some organic basis for limited capacity. Which is a very interesting idea, as the thinking went.

Equal as to looks? Equal as to fate? Let us examine that a little; let us pursue that. Equal as to fate. Of course it is a commonplace remark that

---

15. In the original draft of the Declaration of Independence, circulated by Jefferson and the other members of the drafting committee, there was a 168-word passage on slavery and the slave trade, an accusation against George III, beginning, "He has waged cruel war against human nature itself, violating its most sacred rights of life and liberty in the persons of a distant people who never offended him, captivating & carrying them into slavery in another hemisphere or to incur miserable death in their transportation thither." The precise sequence of events by which the anti-slavery clause was stricken from the final version of the Declaration is not entirely clear, though Jefferson later wrote that Georgia and South Carolina were adamantly opposed to the clause and ending the slave trade, and other northern states involved in the trade had their own reservations (Thomas Jefferson, *Writings* [New York: Library of America, 1984], 22).

16. In the final version of the Declaration, the concluding item in the list of grievances against King George III, begins, "he has excited domestic insurrections amongst us." Most scholars believe this is a reference to the November 1775 proclamation by Lord Dunmore, the last royal governor of Virginia, that enslaved men who joined the British forces would be manumitted. So rather than being even ambiguously an anti-slavery document, the Declaration in its final form opposed any interference with the institution of slavery.

everybody dies. One by one the duties end; one by one the lights go out. But is that a basis for equality? Would you rest your case on that? Equality as to fate. Or do we mean when we say "equality as to fate" equality as to, a . . . how to say this . . . as to the structure of events that take place in an individual's life. All men are involved in joy and in sorrow, in happiness and unhappiness, in sickness, in reverses, in gains and losses. And perhaps it is true that if I am ever able to stand within the context of my own joy and become aware of you in the context of your joy, then the equality that exists between us is an equality that transcends the mathematical thing, but becomes an equality of experience. What about that? When I say that—that suffering unites people, that suffering bottoms this judgment that men are equal, is that valid for you? What do you think? Would you say at once that there are some people who do not suffer in quite the way that I suffer? Do you ever say that I know that you are having a hard time, but you don't know anything about a hard time? You see? I may say that. And I always feel that there is something unique about my kind of hard time that separates me from you. And whenever you talk about my hard time, I say well that's all right for you to say, but you don't stand where I stand, you don't sit where I sit, you don't know what this is. Well, what do you think of that?

Equality of infinite unworthiness? What about that? A whole theological dogma has been built on that. All men are sinners. All men stand in the immediate need of the grace of God. All men are involved in that which in some of its characteristics must of necessity be diabolical and demonic. And that we are bound together by sin. "I was born in iniquity and in sin did my mother conceive me."[17] But the curious thing about the doctrine of equality based upon the notion of infinite unworthiness or infinite depravity or total depravity is the fact that always under all circumstances the individual who is involved in the mire which involves us all is in many ways, and is, in some important ways, trying to get out of it. He is trying to clean himself up, he is trying to get saved, in other words. Now the logic of that is that if I get saved, then at once I break this thing of equality that binds me to all men as the result of my depravity, I become something else, lifted out of that class. And the moment then I

---

17. Psalm 51:5.

decide that I can't be lifted out of that class by myself, but that I can only be lifted out of that class by an act of God, by the Divine Law, by an act of grace, by an "act of election," as Calvin puts it; then it means that in some inscrutable manner I have been elected and you haven't.[18] I didn't choose to be elected. God nodded to me and made me one of the elect, and God sees, therefore, something of merit in me that is infinitely superior to anything in you. And therefore, that doctrine can become at once the basis of all kinds of cults of inequality and doctrines of racial supremacy, rooted in a theology that binds all men together in total depravity.[19] But there is comfort in the fact that everybody is down there with you. [Laughter] There's comfort in the fact.

Now, what then do we mean by equality? What do you think? Perhaps when we say that all men are created equal, we mean something very special and very general and very universal. Have you ever seen little children argue over something—fight? And one of them will say to the other, "I am just as good as you." Have you ever heard a child say that? Just as good as you. Not as good looking as you are, not as economically secure as you are, not as privileged in this way or that way as you are, but just as

---

18. Jean Calvin (1509–1564), the prominent Protestant reformer, was an advocate of the doctrine of predestination. Calvin believed that salvation was God's preordained plan, and that unconditional election is but one aspect of God's providential wisdom and grace. See John Calvin, *Institutes of the Christian Religion* II, 1–7, "Of the Eternal Election, by Which God Has Predestinated Some to Salvation, And Others to Destruction," *The Library of Christian Classics*, ed. John T. McNeill; trans. and indexed by Ford Lewis Battles (Philadelphia: Westminster Press, 1960), 920–32.

19. For a similar argument, see "The Fascist Masquerade," *PHWT*, 3: 158. Thurman argues that there exists a peculiar relationship between a "cult of inequality" and Christian faith within American culture, and that this relationship, as practiced by the American church, adheres to a doctrine of salvation, based on a notion of human depravity, which makes a distinction between those elected by God for salvation and others who are not so favored. It is an easy association, according to Thurman, to create a fictitious relation between divine election and other doctrines of white supremacy that perpetuate a false view of group rights and privileges. He felt that the embrace of practices of inequality within the church is a telling documentary of the church's impotency regarding the moral mandate of "the religion of Jesus." See Walter Earl Fluker, "Howard Thurman's Vision of National Community," in *The Human Search: Howard Thurman and the Quest for Freedom: Proceedings of the Second Annual Thurman Convocation (Martin Luther King, Jr., Memorial)*, ed. Mozella G. Mitchell (Bern, Switzerland: Peter Lang, 1992).

good as you. What is he talking about? What does he mean? What do you mean when you say that? Are you talking in terms of ethics or morality, or are you talking in terms of another kind of value? It is very curious to me, and I mustn't take this on at all, how again and again the human mind tends to seize upon one particular thing as either the solution of all problems or the cause of all difficulties. It's very interesting how we do that.

In *Moby Dick*, Ahab was trying to catch the White Whale. If he destroys the White Whale, then he will destroy all evil. We don't have to go all the way back to Ahab. That's what we're doing now, isn't it? We say, if we can get rid of communism in the world, then we will have destroyed all the evil in the world. One evil, one solution. Now when we begin to think in terms of the meaning of equality personally, one thing we are sure of, and that is that we are never willing to accept any other man's judgment of that which shall be the decisive basis for determining whether we are equal. That's a long sentence, let me say that again. We are never willing to accept any other man's judgment for what is to be the basis of equality.

You remember the fable of the lion and the hunter. They came through the forest and they came to the edge of the forest arguing about who was the greatest or something. The man said, "Of course, I am, for I am the greatest thing on earth." The lion said, "Of course, I am." Then they saw a statue dedicated to some hunter. There it was, a dead lion and a man standing with his foot on his head leaning on his gun. The man said, "See, I told you." Then the lion in the fable said, "But you see, a man made the statue."[20] You see, I am never willing to accept your appraisal of what is meant by my equality. You see?

Therefore, it seems that ultimately the only basis for equality is the equality of infinite worth as seen by me, the individual of infinite worth. When I say that I am as good as you, what I am really saying—and this may sound mystical as some of you have said to me when we talked—but what I really mean is that my life is rooted in a kind of awareness of my meaning that does not arise from your interpretation of my significance, and that nothing, that no judgment that you impose upon me, no order

---

20. "The Lion and the Man Disputing," in *Aesop's Fables*, trans. Laura Gibbs (Oxford: Oxford University Press, 2002), 95–96.

of society into which you seek to have me regimented, can sever my roots from the dimension of awareness that gives to me my inner significance.

Now that may sound to you as if it is nothing, you know? But that is what you mean when you say that you are as good as anybody else. As soon as you look around you, if you mean qualities, possessions, talents, gifts, if you mean those things, all you need to do is look around you, and you can see that from where you sit you can make your case. What do you do? You do not deny the validity of your relationships, but bring to your relationships the integrity of some awareness that is grounded in something that is far more important to you than whether you live or die, than whether life lives or dies, than whether your civilization lives or dies, than whether your country lives or dies.

And that is why the religious man insists that the ultimate meaning of equality is to be found in man's spiritual grounding of his life. And, so, we give up this or that freedom, we give up this privilege or that privilege, we make this compromise or that compromise, in order that we might be able to continue living or doing this or that. But the one thing that we cannot give up, it is not in our power to give up, and that is, in the deepest sense of the word, our own inner[21] sense. Each man [is] of infinite worth to himself, [and] he will not permit any other man to deal with him as if he were of no value. That becomes the basis of whatever morale we may have in our faith in the democratic dogma.

---

21. At this point the extant audio transcription breaks off, but the remainder of the sermon is included in the transcription.

THE DECLARATION OF INDEPENDENCE II: LIFE—AN INALIENABLE RIGHT

August 12, 1951
Fellowship Church

In the second[1] of the extant sermons Thurman delivered on the Declaration of Independence, Thurman devotes his sermon to the first element of the famous phrase "life, liberty, and the pursuit of happiness." There were few concepts more central to Thurman's religious thinking than the idea and the reality of life. And for Thurman, as he argues here, "life" had two primary meanings: individual, creaturely, physical existence, on the one hand, and, on the other, something shared by all living things outside of the specific existence of one's life. As early as 1944 he expressed what would become a favorite cryptic tautology, that "life is alive," explaining it: "If the source of life is alive, then it follows that life itself is alive — even more alive than any particular manifestation of life ... It is an utterly astounding fact that life is alive. Trees die, animals and men die, and so forth; but trees do not disappear, man and animals do not disappear ... The aliveness of life is one of its chief characteristics—in fact, it is the dominant characteristic of life."[2] Thurman's

1. Thurman calls this sermon the third in the Declaration of Independence series; but it is the second extant sermon, and we have no evidence that there is a missing sermon. This sermon exists in three versions: the original tape recording of the sermon, available at the Howard Thurman virtual listening room, at http://archives.bu.edu/web/howard-thurman/virtual-listening-room; a transcription of the sermon, available in Box 11, Folder 2, Item 13, HTC; and a version that appeared in Fellowship Church's magazine, *The Growing Edge* (Fall 1951). Thurman revised his sermon for its appearance in print, and the editors have used this as the authoritative text, though preserving, in places, the oral character of the sermon as originally delivered.

2. "The Cosmic Guarantee in the Judaeo Christian Message" (June 1944). Thurman reworked this for publication as "Judgment and Hope in the Christian

43

thinking was influenced by the vitalism and purposive evolutionism of one of his chief resources, the South African writer Olive Schreiner, who wrote, quoted in Thurman's anthology: "The Universe has become one, a whole, and it lives in all its parts."[3]

In contrast to this expansive view of life, in this sermon Thurman rejects John Locke's notion of individual life as private property, arguing that this separation of living things into totally private existences is a false description of the natural world. It is also a basis of evolution that emphasizes the "survival of the fittest" rather than an ethic that "demands the support for the lives of the meekest and weakest among us" and that the healthy place their health "at the disposal of the sick individual . . . in order that that which is totally vital may continue to be." Moreover, if an individual sees their life as personal property, then, like other forms of private property it becomes something to preserve at all costs. One's life becomes a perpetual hostage to any threat that challenges "the continuation of my body; I will sell anything—honor, integrity, character—anything" to preserve it."[4] Seeing the body as private property also supports a vision of life in which taking of other lives is all too easily justified by

---

Message," reprinted in *PHWT*, 2: 242–47. For a fuller and more mature exposition of the theme of "the aliveness of Life," see *The Search for Common Ground,* a philosophical exposition of the nature of community; Thurman's "Convocation Address," Pittsburgh Theological Seminary (November 1971); and his Mendenhall Lecture "Community and the Will of God" (February 1961). In *The Search for Common Ground,* he writes: "The potential in any given expression of life is actualized and becomes involved in this very process in the actualizing of the potential of some other form of life upon which it is dependent. The cycle is endless, and the integration of any form cannot be thought of as independent of a similar process in other forms. Here is structural dependency expressive of an exquisite harmony—the very genius of the concept of community" (34).

3. Olive Schreiner, quoted in Thurman's anthology of her writings, *A Track to the Water's Edge: The Olive Schreiner Reader,* ed. Howard Thurman (New York: Harper & Row, 1973), 151. For Schreiner's vitalism, see Hannah R. Tracy, "Willing Progress: The Literary Lamarckism of Olive Schreiner, George Bernard Shaw, and William Butler Yeats" (PhD diss., University of Oregon, 2009). Both Schreiner, as in the quote above, and Thurman, at times, argued that in some sense everything in the universe, including supposedly inanimate objects, are also in some sense alive. For Thurman's (and Schreiner's) sometime hylozoism, see Eisenstadt, *Against the Hounds of Hell,* 357–58.

4. Thurman had written about the dangers of private property and treating oneself as property by 1937, in a more political context—property becomes sacred only when it has already become private, and when property becomes sacred, personality becomes secular" ("The Significance of Jesus III: Love," in *PHWT*, 2: 60–67, at 64).

the elastic rationale of "self-defense" or "defense of national honor or alleged destiny." For "whatever may be the extenuating circumstances, the human spirit is deeply penalized when it engages in the taking of life, particularly human life."

Rather than taking another life to preserve your own private existence, Thurman asks, to protect life itself, "under what circumstances is a continuation of your physical existence trivial? . . . For the preservation of which you will, with enthusiasm, lay down your life?" As a pacifist and advocate of nonviolence, this had long been a deep concern of Thurman.[5] In this sermon, he challenges his listeners to try to enter "the upper level of the creative adventuring of the human spirit" to preserve life and ask themselves "which is the more real, to me: my physical life or the loss of my soul?" Life, for Thurman, even when we are willing to surrender it for a higher purpose, remains inalienable.[6]

I want to take the liberty this morning as the third in our series on the spiritual basis or foundation of the Declaration of Independence to read as a background, a short, comparatively short, statement, called "The First Robin," by Haywood Broun.[7] The spirit of this, the insight here is a thing to which I am calling your attention especially, and you, will find the insight. I will not point it out. And that is much better:

---

5. See "The Significance of Jesus V and VI" (1937), in *PHWT*, 2: 74–92, and Eisenstadt, *Against the Hounds of Hell*, 178–83.

6. Arguably, when the Declaration's authors closed the document by pledging to "support this Declaration, with a firm reliance on the protection of divine Providence, we mutually pledge to each other our Lives, our Fortunes, and our sacred Honor," if not quite using Thurman's language, they were expressing something akin to Thurman's main point in this sermon. The struggle to preserve life, liberty, and equality required a religious conception of life more generous, capacious, and collective than life seen as mere personal property.

7. "The First Robin," in Haywood Broun, *Collected Edition of Haywood Broun*, ed. Haywood Hale Broun (New York: Harcourt Brace, 1941 [orig., 1934]), 308–10. Haywood Broun (1888–1939) was a newspaper columnist who supported many liberal and progressive causes. "The First Robin" was a favorite reading of Thurman; see *PHWT*, 4: 317–23, at 322n1.

"York, Pennsylvania, with the temperature at ten degrees below zero, the first robin of the year was seen in York today. It was found dead on Penn Common."

That's the end of the quotation. Call me an old sentimentalist if you will, but this seems to me to be the most tragic news note of the cold wave. I like people better than robins, and there has been widespread and agonizing suffering. But you see, this was the first robin. He was by all odds the pioneer of his clan. He flew up from the south days, weeks, and months before any reasonable robin weather was to be expected.

Without doubt, the rest tried to discourage him. They spoke of the best recorded experience of bird-kind. "Rome wasn't built in a day," some other robin told him. And no doubt he was advised that if he insisted on such precipitous action, he would split the group and no good could come of it.

Somehow, I seem to hear him say, "If ten will follow me, I'd call that an army. Are there two who will join up, or maybe one?"

But the robins all recoiled and clung to their little patches of sun under the southern sky. "Later maybe," they told him, "not now. First, there must be a campaign of education."

"Well," replied the robin, who was all for going to York, Pennsylvania, without waiting for feathery reinforcement, "I know one who will try it. I'm done with arguments, and here I go."

He was so full of high hopes and dedication that he rose almost with the roar of a partridge. For a few seconds, he was a fast-moving speck up above the palm trees. And then you couldn't spot him even with field glasses. He was lost in the blue and flying for dear life.

"Impetuous, I call it," said one of the elder statesmen, while someone took him a worm.

"He always did want to show off," announced another, and everybody agreed that no good would come of it.

As it turned out, maybe they were right. It's pretty hard to prove that anything has been gained when a robin freezes to death on Penn Common. However, I imagine that he died with a certain sense of elation: none of the rest thought he could get there, and he did. The break in weather turned out to be against him; he just guessed wrong in that one respect. And so, I wouldn't think of calling him a complete failure.

And so, when the news gets back home to the robins who didn't go, I rather expect they'll make him a hero. The elder statesman will figure that since he's dead, his ideas can't longer be dangerous, and they cannot deny the lift and the swing of his venture.

After all, he was the first robin. He looked for the Spring, and it failed him. Now he belongs to that noble army of first robins.

Many great names are included. The honors of office and public acclaim of ribbons and medals, the keys of the city . . . these are seldom the perquisite of man or birds in the first flight. These go to the fifth, sixth, and even twentieth robins.

It is almost a rule that the first robins die alone on some bleak common before mankind will agree that he was a hero. And sometimes it takes fifty years, and often a hundred years.

John Brown, Galileo, and those who sought goals before the world was quite ready, are in good standing.

The man who says, "That would be swell but of course, you can't do it," is generally as right as rain. But who wants to get up and cheer for frustration?! In the long haul, the first robin is more right than any. It was his idea. He softened the way for others, and with him, even failure is his own kind of triumph.

He is not the victim of dry rot or caution or doomed eyestrain from too close attention to ledgers.

"Here I go," he cries, and I wouldn't be surprised if he told that the first minute of flight is reward enough, no matter what follows.

And so, in a metaphorical way of speaking, I bear my head and bow low in the general direction of the ice-covered plain, which is known as Penn Common, and I think the brief address should bear the statement: "You are the first, and after you will come others, they will inherit the grubs and the nests and the comfort. But yours is the glory. You are the first robin."

Life as an inalienable right; life as a natural right; life as a universal right. It is interesting that life appears in the Declaration of Independence as one of the rights: the right to life. And the document starts out with a very simple meaning for life, but as the significance of the concept begins to work its way as leaven through the body of the Constitution, the concept of life widens and deepens.

There are two aspects which, concerning which I want you to think this morning. And the first is the initial idea in the Declaration of Independence, which has to do with the relationship, the intimate relationship, between what Locke[8] calls the mind, the spirit, and the body that houses the mind and the spirit.[9] And the body is regarded, as you may recall, the body is regarded as a private property: the property right, the property [or] possession of the mind and the spirit which that body houses or covers or protects.[10] Life, then, is that delicately balanced rela-

---

8. The English philosopher John Locke; see "The Declaration of Independence: Equality," printed in the current volume.

9. Thurman is particularly concerned with the relationship of mind, body, and spirit in the evolution of the human organism and seeks to demonstrate its empirical workings of interdependability and interrelatedness with other living phenomena. The human organism, according to Thurman, reveals an evolutionary process characterized by directiveness and purpose. The emergence of mind, for Thurman, may be a product of the species' response to the history of the organism itself. The human mind does directly and deliberately what nature has done through ages of trial and error. He suggests that the "mind as mind" evolved from the body as part of the unfolding process of potential resident in life, and that mind as such is the basis for the evolution of "spirit." The imagination as mind-evolved spirit continued the same inherent quest for community which is resident in nature and the body. See Mendenhall Lectures, III, "Community and the Prophet's Dream" (February 1961), 1, HTC. Thurman argues that when an individual consciously seeks community, therefore, she or he will discover that "what he is seeking deliberately is but the logic of meaning that has gone into his creation" (HT, *The Search for Common Ground*, 34). See also Walter Earl Fluker, *They Looked for a City* (Lanham, MD: University Press of America, 1988), 32.

10. The English philosopher John Locke in his "Second Treatise of Government" (1689) argued that "though the earth, and all inferior creatures, be common to all men, yet every man has property in his own person," in *Two Treatises of Government and A Letter Concerning Toleration* (New Haven, CT: Yale University Press, 2003), 111. As Thurman suggests, many commentators on Locke have linked his idea of self-ownership to his notion of personal identity developed in *An Essay concerning Human Understanding* (1689). The idea of self-ownership continues to be vigorously debated by contemporary political philosophers. For a recent critique, see G. A. Cohen, *Self-Ownership, Freedom and Equality* (Cambridge: Cambridge University Press, 1995).

tionship that obtains when the mind, the spirit, remains accommodated in the body. Now if for some reason that intimate primary relationship is broken up and the house is vacated, then in its most elemental sense life discontinues; we may say that such a person has died. The interest in the person, the interest in the body, as expressed in the Constitution and in the Declaration of Independence, is an interest that is rooted in the primacy of the relationship between this body, this property, and that which this body, this property, protects: namely, the mind, the spirit, the life. Now let's look at that for a little.

Life seems to me sometimes to be something separate and distinct from me. And I don't know if it seems that way to you; does it sometimes? That life is apart from me; I reflect upon it, I watch its movement, its manifestation, always as an observer. And yet, there is another sense in which life seems to be a part of the fabric of my nature. I remember— if you pardon a personal reference—when I took a basal metabolism test once, and I was curious to find out from the doctor, what does this mean?[11] What is a basal? Now, of course, what I am going to say to you now is what has happened to his explanation after he gave it to me, so he's not responsible. [Laughter] But this is the way it seems as I think about it. He said that a basal is our attempt to find out as nearly as possible what is your rate of living—*your rate of living*. So that's why you rest all night and do these other things, and then you dramatize a kind of slow picture movement to get from your house down to the doctor's office, and then you get there and he lets you lie down for another half hour and rest, and then you put this thing on. [Laughter] Now it is an effort to find out as nearly as possible the amount of oxygen that is consumed when you are just pulsing. And that is your rate of living.

Now, there is something very fierce and very tough and very rugged about the way in which life (whatever life is) infuses the organism and keeps it throbbing. It seems to gather within the confines of the organism a vast resourcefulness. It yields its prerogative inch by inch unless something so fundamental has taken place in the mind—in the organism itself—that this urgency is relaxed; that it subsides, refuses to ener-

---

11. A basal metabolism test, common in the middle decades of the twentieth century, was a test for the rate of oxygen consumption and caloric use for a person in a fasting and resting state. It was often used for persons with issues with their weight.

gize structures—the result, exhaustion. Life in that sense is rooted in the kind of resourcefulness that fights for its continuation, for its persistence, without particular reference to the desires that may be operating in the spirit. My reason may be completely dethroned, so that as far as any of the reflective processes of my mind and spirit are concerned, all is reduced to zero. And yet I will eat and digest my food. I may sink back into the arms of an elemental respiration that will keep me going long after the house is dark and all the windows sealed and the curtains pulled. We call it "coma."

Individual life seems to draw upon an apparently everlasting pulsation that is not under the specific control of any individual mind, that never seems to be uniquely the flavor—the character—of my living and my thinking. It is this universal ground of pulsation—this urgency, this universal and rhythm and respiration—that has caused men to know that life cannot die. You may kill its manifestation at a particular point in time and space, but life cannot die. This is the clue to the sense of mystery and reverence that surround life. It is this gross sense of reverence that is metaphysical in character, that causes men, again and again, to have reverence for *life*, but often have little regard for how they treat life. Reverence for *life*, but no *regard* for life.[12] It is the mass push of life itself that carries with it the vast meaning of reverence. The individual who is aware

---

12. Thurman is echoing Albert Schweitzer's notion of "the reverence for life." Schweitzer popularized the idea of reverence for life as an ethical demand that meant a type of ethics that would reconcile egotism and altruism by demanding respect for all human beings and by seeking the highest development of each individual. Schweitzer believed reverence for life was the highest calling of human beings, and because all are a part of life that exhibits what he called "will-to-live," then it is our moral obligation to participate as expressions of that life and to hold in reverence the high calling that life itself has placed upon us. Schweitzer's, like Thurman's ethical perspective, is born out of a deeply spiritual reflection on and involvement in nature, in which all living beings, human and nonhuman, participate. Schweitzer writes: "ethics consist in my experiencing the compulsion to show to all will-to-live the same reverence as I do my own. *A man is truly ethical only when he obeys the compulsion to help all life which he is able to assist, and shrinks from injuring anything that lives.* If I save an insect from a puddle, life has devoted itself to life, and the division of life against itself has ended. Whenever my life devotes itself in any way to life, my finite will-to-live experiences union with the infinite will in which all life is one" [emphasis added] (Albert Schweitzer, *Reverence for Life* [New York: Harper & Row, 1969], 68). See also HT, "Albert Schweitzer," in *Moral Struggle and the Prophets*, 11–18.

of that reverence recognizes the fact that he can't destroy life. He can only make your little life disappear, but it will come up over there, so why be bothered much about killing, about killing *a* man? And that's the logic of that. Unless it happens to be *you*. Then that's not so good. You see?

The logic of man's experience with life guarantees that life must be protected, in proportion to its privacy, its personal character. There appear then, in established law, provisions for protecting life. The most persistent condition under which it is lawful for one man to take an individual's life is the condition that obtains when his life is being threatened by the other. Self-defense, it is called. Thus, if you are trying to kill me, then in my effort to keep you from doing that I kill you. I am without guilt, under the statutes. Interesting, isn't it? But if an agreement can be worked out, under which there is a collective decision that if human beings behave in a certain way, then the right to take life without guilt is honored. This happens in war. That is why, always, when nations fight, it is very necessary that some kind of philosophy or some kind of rationalization be worked out to protect each side from personal guilt, when in defense of national honor or alleged destiny there must be ruthless destruction of life. Of course, this is an illusion, as post-war problems make evident. Whatever may be the extenuating circumstances, the human spirit is deeply penalized when it engages in the taking of life, particularly human life.

But there is another sense in which I want you to look at life, and I'll stop in a few minutes. Under what circumstances would you gladly give up your life? Let's not hurry over that question. Under what circumstances would you? It is comparatively simple, not altogether easy, but comparatively simple to give up your life once, to die once. Every person who's seated here before me this morning has died many times, not once, but many times. Each time you yielded some of your life you did it on behalf of something which to you [was more important][13] than what you gave up. What was it?

Under what circumstances is a continuation of your physical existence trivial? Under what circumstances? With what kind of issue must you be faced? What must be at stake? For the preservation of which you will, with enthusiasm, lay down your life? Anything? Or is your physi-

---

13. Conjectural insertion.

cal existence so precious to you that regardless of the challenge and the demands, you will choose to keep on breathing and let the values go? What about it? It is not academic, my friends, because we face it daily; always we are involved in this sort of process. Some of us are doing now, on the basis of clear-eyed planning and conviction, certain things which may mean the destruction of our physical existence. We do them with a kind of joy, enthusiasm, and inspiration because we believe that it is better that our physical existence shall disappear rather than the things on behalf of which we lay down our lives shall perish. If you are not involved in that kind of process, you are already dead. Dead.

Let us pursue this one more step. In the whole development of the idea of biological evolution, one of the problems that is created for morality and ethics and for the sensitive religious spirit is that which arises over the significance of the healthy—the fit individual. It seems as if, in the development of life on this planet, the important thing has been to place a premium upon that particular expression of life that is the most perfect manifestation at a particular level.

A crude illustration: The healthiest cat should be the connecting link to carry the torch of life, at the level of cats. The cats that aren't so healthy, in which the torch of life is having a hard time to keep, seem to be eliminated. "Let them be eliminated," life seems to echo. It says, "concentrate on the most perfect expression of the life urge at that level, so that that which is transmitted may be the clearest channel, the largest opening, so that life may continue on the most creative and significant level."

Now when an ethic is introduced, and particularly when the Christian ethic is introduced, it seems it works against this moral insight. Jesus insisted upon the importance of the individual. The greater the need of the individual, the more neglected the individual is, the more he has that is raw and exposed, the greater must be the care and the tenderness with which he must be treated. The Christian ethic demands with utter urgency that we put at the disposal of the sick individual the health that is yours in order that that which is totally vital may continue to be. In behaving thus, we seem to be acting contrary to the very process by which life persists on the planet.

But when we look into it a little more deeply, we may discover that when [a person gives up his life] because it is better that beauty remain than ugliness . . . it is because he is persuaded that that which is trans-mitted—that which will go on to the next generation—is for him of supreme value. To him it is the clearest, the most authentic expression of the dreams and the hopes of the human spirit. He cannot be the agent for passing on the weak, the defiled, the less rather than the highest. It is better to die than to do this. Here again, on the upper level of the creative adventuring of the human spirit, that which seems to be true on the basic biological level gets its validation in an amazing and fascinating and excit-ing manner.

Therefore, when I say that life is a right, I mean more than the con-tinuation of my physical existence. It may not be important whether I live or die. It is important that the dreams that disturbed my mind and quicken my spirit do not perish; that the dreams to which, when I [am] most myself, I have yielded with enthusiasm and conviction be passed on through me with ever-increasing fulfillment. It is better that I shall live thus than I shall continue living, eating, sleeping, and breeding. Until I am ready to make that kind of choice, until I am willing to live my life at that dimension, then if you can jeopardize the security that guarantees the continuation of my body, I will sell anything—honor, integrity, char-acter—anything. What would I give in exchange for my life? Which is the more real to me: my physical life or the loss of my soul?

What about you?

The Declaration of Independence III: Liberty

August 19, 1951
Fellowship Church

In this sermon Thurman continues his argument from the previous week's sermon on life against John Locke's notion that one's life is personal property, and that government's most basic obligation is the protection of private property. If so, Thurman argues "the logic of that is that the less government you have the better . . . just the barest minimum to guarantee the preservation of property rights." This Jeffersonian notion of limited government would include the protection of "private property" in enslaved persons, though Thurman does not mention this.

Liberty and freedom, Thurman argues, are based on the protection of an individual's autonomy. (Unlike elsewhere, Thurman here does not make a distinction between liberty and freedom.)[1] Liberty is not license, the total absence of external coercion, because "absolute freedom, with no limitations, is the most terrifying kind of tyranny." And this is because freedom or liberty, as he argues elsewhere, is having a sense of alternatives; and when none of the alternatives really matters, you are not really experiencing freedom. It is only "with reference to the relationship between the movable and that which at the moment seems to be the immovable that I get the sense of play which is freedom." This is freedom as discipline, and therefore, for Thurman, "your greatest moment of freedom comes when you have faced what for you is the most radical and thoroughgoing test for your life in the light of which the real character of yourself is revealed." The ultimate alternative is to choose the moment of one's death, and this can be preferable to a situation in which one is tortured continuously but kept alive. Death "is one vote you can always

---

1. See "America in Search of a Soul," printed in the current volume.

cast, and the casting of that vote is a symbol of your freedom." This is a very difficult notion of freedom, the sort of freedom that could embolden those he was calling in these years the "apostles of sensitiveness," the sort of freedom that would, in a few years, inspire the civil rights advocates who put their lives on the line to advance the freedom of others.[2]

"**D**rop Thy still dews of quietness, till all our strivings cease. Take from our souls the strain and stress, and let our ordered lives confess, the beauty of Thy Peace."[3]

We are so harassed and buffeted by stress and strain: some of it created by our own stupidity; some created by the deep inner confusions and conflicts of our minds and spirits; some of it created by vast conflicts and stresses and strains in which the life of modern man is involved. And on the shore, where we as individuals live, great tidal waves move in to destroy our little homes, our little gardens, our little private hopes and cherished wishes for fulfillment. Stress and strain. How much we know about it. And therefore, it is well that we sit to think and feel each other's presence in the quietness and gather what strength we may from each other's fortitude and each other's courage, to have our common mood of quiet bound together by an overshadowing Presence that is closer to us than breathing, nearer than hands or feet, and against the background of the quietness created by that Presence, we, each one of us, may find new sources of strength, new grounds for hope, fresh lifts to our spirits.

God, our Father, who has involved us so deeply in thy love that we cannot escape thy Spirit, we thank thee; we thank thee, that despite all of the evidence which seems to point toward our being stranded and alone in the struggle of life, that thou dost open up within us quiet outlets of thy spirit and thy reassurance, to the end that we are not alone. We cannot abide any complete and final isolation, and we give thee thanks that

2. For Thurman's writings on this topic, see "The Apostles of Sensitiveness," in *PHWT*, 3: 170–74. Also, HT, *Deep Is the Hunger: Meditations for the Apostles of Sensitiveness* (New York: Harper & Brothers), 195; HT, *Apostles of Sensitiveness* (Boston: American Unitarian Association, 1956).

3. From one of Thurman's favorite hymns, "Dear Lord and Father of Mankind" (1884), text by John Greenleaf Whittier (1807–1892); see *PHWT*, 4: 214n1.

it is so. Simple things. Ordinary things. Quiet, peaceful, joyous things.
O God, our Father, in whose love we take refuge, and whose strength is
our hope, Amen.

We come now to the fourth[4] in a series of our five thinkings together
on the spiritual foundations of the Declaration of Independence. And
once again, I'd like to read a paragraph from Stephen Vincent Benét's
John Brown's Body. The paragraph, the significance of which you will
understand as we move along, it is a quotation of Abraham Lincoln's,
from the lips of Abraham Lincoln:[5]

> Therefore I utterly lift up my hands
> To you [referring to God], and here and now beseech your aid.
> I have held back when others tugged me on,
> I have gone on when others pulled me back
> Striving to read your will, striving to find
> The justice and expedience of this case,
> Hunting an arrow down the chilling airs
> Until my eyes are blind with the great wind
> And my heart sick with running after peace.
> And now, I stand and tremble on the last
> Edge of the last blue cliff, a hound beat out,
> Tail down, and belly flattened to the ground,
> My lungs are breathless and my legs are whipped
> Everything in me is whipped except my will,
> I can't go on, and yet I must go on.

*And Endowed by their creator with certain inalienable rights, among
these rights are Life, Liberty, and the Pursuit of Happiness.*

As with *Life* last Sunday, we shall think today about *Liberty*. Liberty,
Freedom. It is a matter of very great significance to me that the philo-

---

4. This is the third extant sermon in the series.

5. Stephen Vincent Benét, *John Brown's Body* (Garden City, NY: Doubleday,
Doran, 1928), 219–20. Thurman is quoting Benét recreating Lincoln's thoughts in a
dramatic monologue, not the words of Lincoln himself. In context, Lincoln is saying
that in considering the problems he faces as president, his greatest talent is his tenacity,
seeing an issue through to its necessary conclusion. This was a favorite passage of
Thurman, see *PHWT*, 2: 78.

sophical forebearer of the Declaration of Independence, namely, John Locke,[6] the English philosopher, insisted that the purpose, the function of government is to provide a vehicle for the protection of personal property; that men voluntarily enter into agreements, certain formal agreements, under which the economic and social and political life will operate in order that their property may be protected. Now it is instructive to point out at the very beginning that in the philosopher's mind property did not merely include things that are possessed, but in a rather searching manner property included one's body, as we pointed out in an analysis of the meaning of life. That my body is a part of my private and personal property, and therefore, it is within the compass of the notion that the philosopher has about government that included in those things that are protected, those properties that are protected, would be my body, and, therefore it is reasonable to assume that the logic of that is that there must be included in the protection of my body those things which will make for the survival of my body, those arrangements that will give me an equal chance at physical survival—all of that is included in this notion of the preservation of property as the reason for the development of government.

Now, however, the philosopher insisted (and I'll be through with him in a few minutes, don't be bothered), the philosopher insisted that fundamental to this idea of the reason for government in the first place is the deeper notion that the spiritual, the mental thing, that is protected in the body is the thing that has to be free and equal; so that the notion of government, you see, when in the mind of Locke, is structured on a supposition that fundamental to the governmental process, fundamental to the political arrangement, or the social or economic arrangement, is the underlying thing that man is free and is equal.

Now when this whole idea appears in the Declaration of Independence and subsequently in the Constitution and in the Bill of Rights, and so forth, some very interesting things begin to develop, for you see, if the function of government is to provide protection for property rights, pure and simple, and it isn't to do with anything else, it is a protective device. Then that defines the area in which any kind of initiative can take place.

6. For Locke, see "Declaration of Independence II: Life—An Inalienable Right," printed in the current volume.

The logic of that is that the less government you have the better, you see, just the barest minimum to guarantee the preservation of property rights. So that it is very difficult then to introduce into the colonies a federal principle, you see?

Now, the Declaration of Independence had as one of its primary purposes to get rid of England; I mean to get rid of the crown, to be free. They were independent colonies which fitted into this doctrine, this philosophical and political doctrine that had inspired the movement, but here they are, thirteen independent colonies, but how can you get them together to function as one integrated whole, one unit? Now a government, an overall government would be looked upon with suspicion because the function of government is to protect property rights, and, if we have too much government, too centralized, then it starts doing other things. And those other things would include encroaching upon the private, personal prerogatives of the individual. And that is why Thomas Jefferson was afraid of the federal principle, and that is at once some insight into the struggle that went on between Hamilton and Jefferson and Jay[7] over this whole matter of the federal principle. Jefferson was much more on the side of states' rights, and you can see the logic of states' rights; it stems directly from this idea that it is inherent in the Lockean notion about the reason for government in the first place. Now, so much for all of that, by way of background which you may hold in mind or you may dismiss.

There emerges then this insistence upon freedom as one of the rights: freedom as a distinct derivative from the concept of equality of persons. And you may recall when we were talking about equality we insisted that equality ultimately meant that men are equal, equal in their own ultimate worth, in the limitless, boundless potential of significance which at long last a man attaches to himself, that as a unit that is alive he is in touch with a vast meaningful continuum that sustains and supports and

---

7. Alexander Hamilton (1757–1804), John Jay (1745–1829), along with James Madison (1751–1836) were the three pseudonymous authors of the eighty-five articles that appeared in New York newspapers between October 1787 and April 1788, known collectively as the Federalist Papers, urging New York State's ratification of the federal Constitution. Thomas Jefferson (1745–1826) emerged as a chief opponent of Hamilton's efforts to strengthen the power of the federal government, and was a defender of reserving more power to the states.

breathes through his life, and that his relationship with that continuum is a private, personal irrevocable relationship, and no man has a prior prerogative that will infringe upon that equality in that sense.[8]

Now, from that notion of equality there arises a very interesting sense of freedom and liberty. What is liberty? When you say that you are free, what do you mean? Perhaps you don't say that. When you say that you want to be free, what do you mean? Do you mean that you want to do as you wish when you wish it without regard to anything other than your wish? Is it an insistence upon the ultimate character of your own autonomy? Is that what you mean by freedom? Under what circumstances are you willing to yield areas of your freedom? Before what kind of demand will you relax your insistence upon the carrying out of the logic of your primary desires? Will you give up your will to freedom, if by giving up your will to freedom you can be assured that you will have food to eat and a job, that the grounds of your economic life will be sustained and guaranteed? If to be free means that you must give expression to your opinions, for instance, and yet you realize that if you give expression to your opinions that you lose your job, so on behalf of your job do you relax your insistence upon this expression of your freedom in order that the economic security of your life will not be disturbed? Or do you have another name for that? Not giving up freedom, making an adjustment to an inevitable set of circumstances, or some . . . to be reasonable rather than unreasonable, seeing the other fellow's point of view, and the other fellow happens to be the one who is responsible for your job, so you see his point of view and you salute it. [Laughter in congregation]

What do you mean by freedom? Have you thought out the lines along which you must function in order to be free? Which lines are for you so fundamental to the integrity of your person that you are unwilling to relax your insistence upon those, whatever the cost may be? Is there anything like that in your life? Or is the center of your interest in freedom a vacuum so that it doesn't matter what the demand is? You adjust yourself

---

8. See Thurman's discussion of the inherent worth and dignity of the person, which is the basis of a covenantal relationship between the individual and God that grounds the equality of persons: "A Faith to Live By: Democracy and the Individual II," Fellowship Church, October 16, 1952, printed in the current volume.

to that demand quickly because there is nothing informing the character of your concern for freedom except not to be disturbed. Is that it?

This is so important for us. And we have a name for it; we say this individual is an opportunist, that he rides with every wind because the center of his concern for freedom is a vacuum. And if it's a vacuum, then he welcomes into the citadel of control whatever happens to be the prestige-bearing and significant insistence of the moment. So if the insistence is prestige-bearing enough at any particular moment, then it rides in the central place and becomes the control. What about it?

Now the other side of that dilemma is just as cruel, for it may be, you see, that you have at the center of your control, at the center of the core of your urgency toward freedom, something that is so fixed, so hard, so definitive and rigid, that you can only define your freedom in terms of the fulfillment of this particular thing, the fulfillment of this particular set of categories. So what if your sense of freedom has at the center of your core, let us say, being a citizen of the United States? Case in point, it's a good thing to have that. But with that thing riding the saddle as the thing along which your sense of freedom is structured, then the most blessed thing that you can give to all peoples of the world who happen not to be Americans is to make them Americans. Now let your minds for the rest of the week—you've been doing it already, I'm sure—play along this area and see where you are, locate yourself, define yourself.

Now I should like to go on to the third phase of the meaning of freedom, and then I'm through. What does freedom mean? I'd like to make two or three suggestions. The first thing that I suggest is that freedom means a sense of option, a sense of alternative. It may not mean alternatives: it may not mean option, but it always means a sense of option, a sense of alternative. The idea of freedom in that sense [tape skips] . . . you could crawl under the benches, you could play up there where there were all sorts of things, and you were perfectly content to stay here while your mother was having coffee downstairs. But if, in going out of the door when your mother was leaving you here, she said, "Now, Jack, you can only stay in this room. You can't go out in the hall. That is forbidden; don't go out in the hall. You must stay in here with the chairs and the benches and the rest of it."

Now, before she said that, you wondered how long she was going to stay up here talking with you. You wanted her to go on about her business so that you could begin enjoying the room. But after she said that, then you knew that the only way by which you could enjoy this room would be to be sure that you could go out the door if you wanted to. Now freedom, in its essence, means this sense of alternative. It may not be an alternative that I embrace, you see, but the essence of freedom means the intimate, primary, insistent prerogative that I will not yield unless I have found something so tremendous that whether I go in the room or out of the room somehow seems strangely irrelevant and inconsequential.

And that's why death is so important in human life, because you have this final alternative. You can stand just so much, and then all the lights go out. That is why fainting has so creative a role in the enrichment of the personality, because when the point of endurance reaches whatever the word you use for the ultimate thing, then "Phoof" [sound like air coming out a balloon], which means that I cash in on my alternative. But I stand, and stand, and stand as long as I can, acting as I stand as if the only alternative I have is to endure; and finally, the threads of my endurance are exhausted, and there emerges on the horizon another alternative, blacking out as we say, and when I black out, in the doing I affirm the grounds of my freedom.

Much of the march of human progress through the centuries is this quality of endurance. Men sometimes voluntarily precipitate the exercise of the option by doing the things that will take their lives; they become martyrs. Because you can always die, you see; that is one vote you can always cast, and the casting of that vote is a symbol of your freedom. That is the one thing that bottoms all of the sense of freedom which we exercise on more superficial levels or bases. But there is one problem that is created by it. [This happens when] in the hands of vicious men, men who understand with cunning the quiet recesses of the movement and respiration of the human spirit, [who] understanding [its] mechanism, let that understanding inform the intimate character of their brutality. Such men have worked out devices by which they will not let you cast that final vote, and that is a part of the whole diabolic character of, of torture in modern life. Men will be worked up to a certain point, when with all of their passionate endeavor and all of their historic background in life and in living they say, "At last I will exercise the great and crowning act of my personality by choosing the moment when I cast my final vote with my life, and that thing for which I could not live, I gladly die."

Something wonderful about that. But when you are in the hands of people who won't let you die, who will just torture you up to a certain point and then they slide back down the hill and then come up around the other side; and they don't ever get to that line, so you can't ever cast that vote. You see? Then your freedom becomes something else; it becomes the exercise of another kind of alternative which does not take into account the fact that the guarantee of your freedom is the casting of this final vote. Now I can't pursue that further this morning, but I will. What happens when alternatives of that character are denied you? What happens to your spirit? What happens to your mind, when you are not permitted to die, even though to die would be to exercise this final option that would give to you a sense of freedom?

Now freedom means something else too. It means that there is at the core of it this experience, this notion, this push, a very strange contradiction, a discipline. Discipline. And the notion of freedom stands over against the notion of discipline, you see?[9] That is why if freedom were absolute, if you had an absolute freedom, if you could do as you pleased, if you could give full expression to that which you desire, if there were no limitation, then you would be a slave. Think about it before you disagree with me. Absolute freedom, with no limitations, is the most terrifying kind of tyranny. It is with reference to the relationship between the movable and that which at the moment seems to be the immovable that I get the sense of play which is freedom.

Have you ever seen a little child—I keep coming back to that—who had a gun? I mean one of these playthings, and drums, and bicycle, and everything that his heart could wish Santa Claus brought him? He sits down Christmas morning in the midst of everything, every conceivable

---

9. At another place, Thurman writes, "The secret is the quiet inner purpose and release of vitality with which it inspires the act. Achieving the goal is not measured by some external standard, though such must not be completely ignored. Rather, it is measured in terms of *loyalty* to the purpose and the freedom which it inspires" [italics added]; HT, "Freedom Is a Discipline," in *The Inward Journey* (New York: Harper & Brothers, 1961), 63.

desire that his little heart could muster and bursts out crying with desolation. He plays the drum, he blows his horn, he eats candy, he cracks nuts, he takes a ride on the scooter, he rides on his bicycle. We can't take it. There must be at the core of freedom that which announces the dignity of the human spirit, and what is that dignity? That dignity is that it has a prior right to live and function with discrimination. When that right is cut off because it is surfeited, then the human spirit languishes and dies. Therefore, your greatest moment of freedom comes when you have faced what for you is the most radical and thoroughgoing test for your life, in the light of which the real character of yourself is revealed; and once you have had that kind of stripping, it is then that your sense of self becomes operative and you function as a free person because at last you know what it is for which you will live with your life and against which you will live with your life. Your freedom is found in the intimate relation between the judgment that is yours when you make that kind of choice. I ask you finally, then, if your freedom is measured in terms of the clarity with which you know what it is you will live your life with your life and against what it is you will live with your life. If that is yours, then you are free; you are free in the most searching way that freedom counts. It is very interesting and very terrifying because you can always be mistaken.

THE DECLARATION OF INDEPENDENCE IV: THE PURSUIT OF HAPPINESS

August 26, 1951
Fellowship Church

In the final sermon in his series on the Declaration of Independence, Thurman turns to the last element in the famous triad in its preamble, the peculiar eighteenth-century phrase "the pursuit of happiness." Thurman suggests that the phrase "pursuit of happiness" was a substitution for John Locke's notion of property as a fundamental right, and humorously tries to reconstruct Thomas Jefferson's thought processes in arriving at the phrase. However, the phrase, or close variants thereof, was fairly common in eighteenth-century political writings, as in Virginia's Declaration of Rights, adopted only a month before the ratification of the Declaration of Independence, which spoke of, in addition to the right of "the means of acquiring and possessing property," the right of "pursuing and obtaining happiness and safety." Pauline Maier has suggested that the phrase would have been equivalent to the common invocation in eighteenth-century America of Micah 4:4: "they shall sit every man under his vine and fig tree; and none shall make them afraid."[1] If so, this would be very similar to Thurman's understanding of citizenship, which can only be exercised from a place of security, with protection against arbitrary violence and systematic exploitation.[2] For Thurman, the "pursuit of happiness," as with many commentators, is a collective right, one that builds on the right to life and liberty, and requires "the structur-

---

1. Pauline Maier, *American Scripture: Making the Declaration of Independence* (New York: Vintage, 1997), 134.
2. See HT, *Jesus and the Disinherited* (New York: Abingdon-Cokesbury, 1949), 33–34.

ing of an environment [that] would make it a reasonable thing for man to pursue happiness."³

Happiness, for Thurman, transcends material pursuits of power, position, and prestige, even material necessities like food and clothing; rather, it has to with genuineness or the integrity of the inner life and commitment. Thurman argues that in the America of the 1950s the incessant din of external, commercialized stimuli meant that people were not listening to themselves, and that people had become afraid of silence. The "outer emphasis is so much a part of our lives that if we can't keep talking we are embarrassed, and so we just talk," and empty jabbering has become a substitute for having real conversations.

At the same time, Thurman argues that "neighborliness" is an essential quality of humanity and of "the pursuit of happiness," and this extends beyond individuals and groups to nations and civilizations, and that the United States and European imperial powers, in their selfish pursuit of their own self-interests, have neglected basic questions of justice and compassion to others. "Think of how much happiness the colonial policy of Western civilization has provided for so many generations, to so many people. And at what price? The collective unhappiness of so many millions of people." He closes his sermon, "So, from where we sit then, let us not be so overwhelmed by the apparent collapse of the worlds around us that we don't do the things that are needful, that will redeem our own souls, and perhaps, set up the kind of creative and spiritual process that may save the world," a Declaration of Independence not just for the United States but for all the colonized peoples in the world.

A few years later, Thurman, speaking in Boston, would quote the preamble to the Declaration and claim that it is a kindred "urge to liberty and equality that explains the revolution now taking place among the peoples of Asia and Africa in their efforts to throw off colonial rule and become equal partners in the community of nations."⁴

---

3. On this point, in addition to Maier, *American Scripture*, see Danielle Allen, *Our Declaration: A Reading of the Declaration of Independence in Defense of Equality* (New York: Norton, 2014).

4. HT, "Speech at Lambda Kappa Mu Human Relations Dinner," in *PHWT*, 4: 131. For Thurman and post-war decolonization, see Peter Eisenstadt, *Against the Hounds of Hell*, 308–11.

Often it is very easy to lose our sense of direction, to drift without knowing that we are drifting, or to drift with the awareness that our drifting paralyzes us, so that we cannot do anything about our drifting. It is so hard to draw a line between the confusion within and the confusion without, deep uncertainties within, vast uncertainties without. And all of this makes for bewilderment of mind and a troubling disturbance of spirit. And we turn to the quiet times, always with some measure of hope, that within us the miracle will take place, that we shall experience the bonds for hurt minds, the invasion of redemption that will save us from our sins; always our spirits turn in anticipation that this time it may happen. That what we seek we shall find, that our hunger shall be satisfied. Again and again and again, we knock at the same door.

Yet there is something very wonderful about it, this urge ever to seek, this belief in the validity of peace within and without, this naïve awareness that we are not alone, the child-like confidence that fertilizes the roots of our maturity, that keeps the leaves of trees green, when all around us is barren. O God our Father, we would not seek thee if we had not already found thee. We would not reach out for thy light if thy light was not already burning within us. O God our Father, accept our faith. The quiet thanks of our hearts, the nameless feeling of well-being. This is enough for us, this is enough for us, O God our Father, Amen.

On the spiritual foundations, or the religious foundations, of the Declaration of Independence. I would like to read a few lines from a poem by Richard Dixon,[5] as background for the section which has to do today with the pursuit of happiness:[6]

> There is but one way for thee, but one; inform
> Thyself of it; pursue it, one way each
> Soul hath by which the Infinite in reach
> Lieth before him; seek and ye shall find

---

5. Richard Watson Dixon (1833–1900), Anglican divine and prominent poet, with connections to the Pre-Raphaelite movement.

6. Richard Watson Dixon, "Love's Consolation," in *Christ's Company: And Other Poems* (London: Smith, Elder, 1861), 97.

To each the way is plain; that way the wind
Points all the trees along; that way run down
Loud singing streams; that way pour on and on
A thousand headlands with their cataracts
Of toppling flowers; that way the sun enacts
Its travel, and the moon and all the stars
Soar; and the tides move towards it; nothing bars
A man who goes the way that he should go,
The waves along the strand whiten beyond his eyes; the trees
    tossed back
Show him the sky; or, heaped upon his track in a black wave,
    wind-heaped, point onward still
His one, one way. O joy, joy, joy to fill
The day with leagues! Go thy way, all things say.
Thou hast thy way to go, thou hast thy day
To live; thou hast thy need of thee to make
In the hearts of others; do thy thing, yes.
And be thou sure of this: no other can
Do for thee that appointed thee of God
Not any light shall shine upon thy road
For other eyes
    Thee the angel calls
As he calls others; and thy life to thee
Is precious as the greatest's life can be
To Him; so live thy life and go thy way.

Of course, that is enough to say, and you may decide at the end of the minutes that it would have been very much better, if well enough had been let alone. [Aside by Thurman, probably commenting on the poem.]

We have been thinking together about certain aspects of the Declaration of Independence, the broad assumptions out of which it arose, the false assumptions, the feeling tones, desires, the desperateness, the turmoil, chaos, hope, just a great mixture. It insists that men are created equal, and that all men are endowed by God with certain rights, rights that are given, rights that are part of the very warp and woof of living, a part of the texture of experiencing. In the breakdown in the Declaration of Independence are these rights: life, liberty, and the pursuit of happiness. We thought together about life, and how life means not only gross basic physical existence, but life also means the outreach of the human spirit in terms of values and meanings that may be so significant that on behalf of those values and meanings one would gladly give up one's physical existence. We talked together about liberty, freedom, and what it means in terms of the fulfillment of life.

And now we come to the last of the spelling out on the part of the Declaration, the pursuit of happiness. Everybody is interested in happiness, and I think we are now more interested in happiness today than ever before, because everyone is so tired. It's very interesting. If you stood where I stood and I sat where you sat, to look at the exhausted appearance. [Laughter] Now I'm not being personal, but you look so tired, and weary, and beat down, and I suppose I look the same way to you. [Laughter] It's a part of where we are. Everybody is tired and weary, and looking for happiness. But we don't find it.

The pursuit of happiness. What happened in Thomas Jefferson's[7] mind that made him do this amazing thing? You remember we have been talking about how Thomas Jefferson was deeply influenced by Locke,[8] and his whole concept, and that Locke's trilogy is life, liberty, and property. Those are the rights, you see? And Thomas Jefferson must have had quite a battle, I can imagine it:

"Life, liberty, and property?" No, that doesn't sound right. It is right for me to have my property, but life, liberty, and property? Life, liberty, and property? [said quickly] Life, liberty, and property? [drawn out] Life, liberty, and property? Life, *liberty,* and property? Life, liberty, and *property?* No. Life, liberty, and then we want to round it out. What can I say that would take the heart of life and the heart of liberty, and put in into one creative synthesis of meaning for the human spirit? Ah! Life, liberty, and happiness. No, that isn't it. Life liberty, and happiness. That says something that Jefferson couldn't have said and nobody could have said.

---

7. Thomas Jefferson (1746–1826), primary author of the Declaration of Independence.

8. English philosopher John Locke (1632–1704), whose influence on Jefferson and the writing of the Declaration of Independence was discussed by Thurman in the previous sermons in the Declaration of Independence series.

Life, liberty, and happiness. But life, liberty, and the pursuit of happiness? That's more realistic, isn't it? Or is it? Do you think so? Life, liberty, and the pursuit of happiness? The pursuit of happiness.

The first presupposition, which is very important here, is that [there] can be no guarantee for happiness. No guarantee. No combination of things if put together will automatically net happiness. Now if there can be no psychological guarantee for happiness, then of course it is obvious that there can be no legislative guarantee for happiness. The Declaration of Independence recognizes the pursuit of happiness as one of the rights. That is, if I have a sense of infinite worth, a sense of self that is grounded in this feeling, this continuum of value which with I must always maintain primary contact if my life is to have meaning. If I am regarded as an equal, if I regard myself as an equal of every other man, and if from within the full-orbed awareness of that sense of equality, I can move around in my mind and spirit without being bound, then given those two things, the kind of environment should be created that would make it possible for it to be a reasonable thing for men to pursue happiness. And therefore, in the Declaration of Independence, and in the Bill of Rights, and in various aspects of the Constitution, among all of these words, amendments, [and] statements of one kind or another, . . . words, which have as their purpose, if these words are effective, the structuring of an environment, which will make it a reasonable thing, given these other two generalizations about equality and freedom, to make it a reasonable thing for man to pursue happiness.

What is happiness? Have you ever said I'm happy? Have you ever said that? What did you mean? If you think about it, and if you think very hard about it, I might pick up the overture. What did you mean when you said you were happy? Did you mean you had what you wanted? Or are you happy because life has never given you what you want, and you are so grateful that life is wiser than you are? Like the phrase of Havelock Ellis,[9] now that I'm sixty-five years old, I thank God that God did not answer the prayers of my youth.

---

9. Henry Havelock Ellis (1859–1944) was a pioneering researcher of human sexuality, and the author of books on many topics. The quote was a favorite of Thurman's; see *PHWT*, 3: 285; and HT, *The Way of the Mystics*, 47.

Happiness. What do you mean by it? Let's think about it. If you give your prescriptions, how would it read? Would they have to do with things; with clothes, for instance, not clothes in general, but clothes in particular? Would it have to do with that? Would it have to do with food? Would it have to do with a certain kind of prestige? What is your prescription? Does it have to do with a certain kind of association, that if you would have this kind of association, you would be happy? Does it have to do with place? So that it is unthinkable that you would ever be happy in San Francisco, where there is fog, and you're bound here, and can't go anywhere? Does it have to do with place? Is it located there? And if it is in terms of position, if it is in terms of money, of economic power, if it is in terms of clothes or possessions of one kind or another, or of place, you don't really mean that if you had the money, you would be happy, if you had the clothes you would be happy, if you had the kind of food you wanted you would be happy. Is what you mean that if you had the clothes or the economic power or the place, the location, then it would be reasonable for you to pursue happiness? Is that what you mean? No, it isn't, is it?

It's very simple to be quite iconoclastic about it, that modern man wants money, that's his god, and he wants this and this and this, and those things would make you happy? Have you ever talked to anybody who had the things that you are sure that if you had, you would be happy? And you found that the precious ingredient was missing? That the person hoped that if he could get enough of it, the law of averages would finally bring one load that had the previous ingredient in it?

There are two or three general things about the basis of happiness . . . which you thought about your own private prescription. The first suggestion is that happiness always assumes that the individual has been able to work out an increasingly satisfactory relationship between his inner life and his outer life . . . That is why I can't conceive of a person finding or experiencing the sense of spiritual enlargement—that's what happiness is—who doesn't spend some time by himself. For, you see, we must work out, each person for himself, a satisfying relationship between his inner world and his outer world. And so much of modern life is outer life.

When have you had a good, a satisfying conversation, with somebody? You know, just good, good talk. Not discussing something that brought you together, you know, some issue, or trying to get some decision, but when you had a sense of spiritual enlargement, as you touched the fringes of meaning and significance in another person's life, as you tarried, tarried. When does that happen? When you turn off the radio and long-playing records [laughter] if you're going to have a chance.[10] The outer emphasis is so much a part of our lives that if we can't keep talking we are embarrassed, and so we just talk. Why are we afraid of the inner? We can never be happy until we relate these two, and we can't pursue happiness until we can integrate these two. It is a part of the long, dramatic history of the race, that whenever the spirit of man persists in denying the right, the urgency of his inner life for withdrawal, that he dies. He dies. And every man or woman who has had his imagination kindled and his spirit even inspired diabolically has included in the springs of his validity, retreat, withdrawal, time for sinking the shafts of one's spirit down into lower waters. Hitler would have been destroyed long before the collapse of . . . [No apparent break in the tape, but the thought is unfinished.]

Have you worked out some integration between the outer and inner? Do you ever withdraw? Or are you always involved in the demands of the externals, and you run from one external to the other external, always hoping that you'll find it? Inner and outer. And you can only work out some integration between those by spending time exploring the inner, until at last you discover that the clue to the outer is the inner [bangs pulpit]; and what I seek way out there, I seek it because what I am finding in here. You don't have to be a long-haired mystic, or some curious somebody, but if you just want to be a decent human being, you've got to get those two things together. And the Declaration of Independence felt that if all the obvious things were taken care of, such as protecting your home and your person, your right to live here and there, if all those things that are expressed in the amendments to the Constitution and the Bill of Rights, if all those things were taken care of, then it would be possible to have a normal expectation that human beings would make this creative discovery and creative connection.

---

10. The long-playing record, or LP, which initially held about 22 minutes of music per side, was introduced in the United States in 1948. It rotated at 33 1/3 revolutions per minute (rpm), as opposed to the then-standard 78 rpm records, which could hold only about five minutes of music per side.

There's one final word. The pursuit of happiness can never be at the expense of somebody else's. The pursuit of happiness cannot be at the expense of my neighbor's happiness. Isn't it interesting, when we pause for a moment and [think about] the things that are happening all over the world while we sit here? India is not coming to the peace treaty; all the millions of people of China will not be a part of the peace treaty, the whole Arab world, in complete and terrifying revolt.[11] Think of how much happiness the colonial policy of Western civilization has provided for so many generations, to so many people. And at what price? The collective unhappiness of so many millions of people.

And now, when there is a change of mind and heart in various ways, not altogether but in various ways, on the part of the representatives of Western culture and Western civilization, there is nobody in that part of the world who can hear what they are saying. Because, for so many years, Western civilization pursued its happiness by lining its coffers with the vitals of the colonies. Now today, nobody trusts the heirs of those people who found their happiness at the expense of so much suffering of many other people. And we want to be loved, we want to trust and be trusted, we want peace in the world, and every move we make sends us further away from the dream that instincts the heart. But why does it? Because we didn't realize the thing that I'm saying now. You can't pursue happiness on a private race track. For what you get is not a simple thing like unhappiness, but you get disintegration of soul that requires a kind of spiritual rehauling and rebirthing, if I may put it that way, precisely at the moment when there is a minimum of confidence in the validity of the spiritual life. That's the tragedy and that's the dilemma. Precisely at that

11. Thurman is referencing the difficulties and tensions surrounding the Treaty of San Francisco, also known as the Treaty of Peace with Japan, which was in final negotiation when Thurman delivered this sermon. The treaty was signed by forty-nine nations on September 8, 1951, in San Francisco. The treaty formally ended the American occupation of Japan and restored Japanese sovereignty. Three members of the United Nations, Czechoslovakia, the Soviet Union, and Poland, refused to sign. India and Yugoslavia chose not to send representatives. Italy and China were not invited. It is not clear to whom Thurman was referring by the "Arab revolt," perhaps to the continuing resentment among Arabs and Muslims over the creation of Israel. Thurman's good friend and former Howard University colleague, Ralph Bunche, had been awarded the Nobel Peace Prize the previous year for his role in helping to negotiate the truce agreements that ended the 1948 Arab-Israel War.

moment the only thing that can rehabilitate us is spiritual rebirth. So, from where we sit then, let us not be so overwhelmed by the apparent collapse of the worlds around us that we don't do the things that are needful, that will redeem our own souls, and, perhaps, set up the kind of creative and spiritual process that may save the world. The pursuit of happiness.

A Faith to Live By: Democracy and the Individual I

October 19, 1952
Fellowship Church

In the fall of 1952, Thurman preached eight sermons on the subject of "A Faith to Live By."[1] Topics of the earlier sermons, not printed here, included "faith," "God," "Jesus Christ," and "man." The final two sermons in the series were on democracy. In them, he considers the political, ethical, and religious implications of democracy.[2] In this sermon, Thurman, as he does in other places, contends there is a metaphysical significance to democracy; that it is founded upon the inherent qualities of creativity and dynamism, and its movement toward an ever-unfulfilled goal is at one with the very movement of Life itself. In this, Thurman ascribes the attribute of being alive, a vitalism and a teleological striving, to American democracy. He reasons that for "democracy, one of the basic presuppositions upon which it rests, a metaphysical presupposition, is that this is the kind of world that is grounded in creativity; that it is essentially dynamic; that potentials are an important part of any present consideration or predicament."

One of the key principles of democracy, Thurman argues, is that every individual is an end in himself or herself, and never a means to another end. In true democracy, there is no equality of gifts, talents, or abilities, argues Thurman, but only the "equality of infinite worth." To the extent that democracy works in America, it is because for three hundred years the

---

1. The title of the sermon series is probably derived from Lewis Mumford's chastened evaluation of the prospects for American democracy; Lewis Mumford, *Faith for Living* (New York: Harcourt Brace, 1940).

2. The argument here resembles some of Thurman's later writings on the topic of the meaning of America; see " Freedom under God" (1955), "The American Dream," in *PHWT*, 4: 112–20, 215–20; "America in Search of a Soul," printed in the current volume.

United States has had "the richest cross section of human beings collected anywhere else in the world," and the goal of democracy is to "develop confidence and faith, technique, methodologies for implementing the dream of one world, one family that God has for the human race."

We come now almost to the end of our series Faith for Living. We have one more next Sunday, and we will conclude the series.

Today we are thinking together about democracy, as one of the elements, one of the crucial elements in our faith for living. It is very difficult to talk about this because almost everything that anyone has to say about the meaning of the democratic dogma sounds like an old frayed story [that] we have heard many times. But nevertheless, even at the risk that is involved there, I do want to think as creatively as possible with you about it because the point at which democracy lives or dies is in the human heart, in the human spirit. And however accurate and technically consistent may be the political and the economic structure or blueprint, the implementation of the dogma has much to do with the faith of the people.

So, I'd like to ask you a question this morning: do you believe in democracy? Do you? I remember hearing Reinhold Niebuhr say one day that he believed very much in democracy when he was functioning in his capacity as a professor in Union Theological Seminary. But when he was functioning in his capacity as a member of the board of trustees of the Eden Theological Seminary, he didn't believe very much in democracy.[3] It depends, I suppose. While you are posing that question in your own mind against the context of your own private living, explore with me what seems to be the subsoil, the ground in the technical sense, upon which the whole democratic dream and hope and dogma rest. There are two or three fundamental things to which I call your attention. The first is that either this is a world, a universe in which it is a reasonable thing to have purposes, to have goals, dreams, that sort of thing—or it is not. For if

---

3. See Thurman's lecture series "Mysticism and Social Change," delivered at Eden Seminary in 1939, probably at Niebuhr's behest, in *PHWT*, 2: 190–222. For Thurman's friendship with the prominent theologian Reinhold Niebuhr (1892–1971), see Eisenstadt, *Against the Hounds of Hell*, 176–78.

in its very structure, life is finished, is complete, is rounded out, is whole, or in its very structure life is fluid, dynamic, unfinished, incomplete. Now if it be true that life is finished, complete, rounded out, then all hope about life and its meaning, either private or public, personal or impersonal, which is not a definition of life as it is, is futile. For it means—do you see that you can't basically do anything about anything if the thing is fixed, finished? The only thing, all you can do is wait.

I remember once I went over to Toronto, and from there I went way up 150 miles or 200 miles north to a Canadian student conference.[4] When I was there, two young people were taken ill with polio. We didn't know it. They kept it very quiet. When I came down to Toronto on Saturday morning, I stayed with a friend until Sunday evening. When I finished my work Sunday evening, I got a train and came back to New York and then on to Washington where I was living. I had been in the house about a couple of hours that particular Monday morning when the telephone rang. The person on the other end of the telephone said, "This is the United States Department of Health.[5] We have been informed by the Department of Health of Ontario that you have had a primary exposure to polio and that you escaped across the border without being quarantined." I didn't know anything about it so I said, "Now under such a circumstance what does one do?" He said, "One simply waits, and if you get something, a nose irritation, some sort of head and spine [pain]—then you call me day or night." In the course of twenty-four hours, I had the worst headache—it's almost a terrifying thing to wait when you know that the thing is going to fall, you know what it is, and it is even more terrifying if you don't know.

So, if, you see, life is finished—then fundamentally the human spirit is stripped of all options except those that bear directly on that which is, you see. But if it isn't, if the nature of life is such that life is dynamic, is fluid, is essentially creative, then purposes, aspirations, utopias, if you please, may take on a relevancy to life and where it is going. And to have dreams and hopes and aspirations, purposes, goals not only then becomes

---

4. Probably "The Significance of Jesus," six lectures delivered at YMCA Park at Lake Couchiching, ninety miles north of Toronto, in the summer of 1937; see *PHWT*, 2: 44–92.

5. Then called the United States Public Health Service.

a possibility for the human spirit, but it becomes mandatory. Now democracy, one of the basic presuppositions upon which it rests, a metaphysical presupposition, is that this is the kind of world that is grounded in creativity; that it is essentially dynamic; that potentials are an important part of any present consideration or predicament. Do you see what that means? It means that life and time are both on the side of that which is unfulfilled, that which is on the make, that which has not arrived. So, when the human spirit broods over the stubborn and sometimes unyielding and recalcitrant aspects of chaotic human relations, it does it with confidence that it is possible for the raw materials of experience and of living to be fashioned and refashioned, shaped and reshaped in accordance with great aspiring and great hoping and great dreaming. Now that is one of the basic pillars upon which the whole democratic experience of the race rests.

Now, do you see what that means when you begin to apply it? For democracy insists that you can arrive at a sense of direction, a sense of goals, a collective sense of direction, a collective sense of goal. And if you can establish in your relatedness to people, if you can get a sense of a group experience by individuals in the group, then there will become increasingly available to the group and, therefore, to the individuals who participate in the group experience a wisdom and an insight that no one of them working alone could gather unto himself or herself. So, we hear a great deal about the democratic process, and sometimes it is quite a nuisance because it takes time and often you don't have the time. That is, you don't think you have the time.

I remember once when our younger daughter was just five years old and we were living in Rochester, New York, for the winter, and I wanted to get a train forty-five minutes from that time, and I had to finish a chapter from a book that I had borrowed from the library, and she came rushing into the room wanting me to do something.[6] I don't remember what it was, but it was something that was very urgent, and I said but I can't do it, you see I'm reading, I am studying; I've got to finish this before the taxi comes to take me to the railway station." And she said, "But I want you to do this *now*, Daddy." "But don't you see that I can't do it. You are wasting

<hr>

6. Thurman had a sabbatical at Colgate Rochester Divinity School (his alma mater) in the 1939 spring semester.

my time." And she kept insisting. So, I closed the book for a minute, and I put a new rumble in my voice and just surrounded her with a general climate of violence. I didn't do anything but that, and she bristled, and, being her mother's daughter, she stood her ground and finally rushed out of the room—[turned] her back just like that. Now I thought about it on the train, and I could've worked the democratic process. It was all there. All the raw materials were there. I could first have established a sense of community in another dimension. With a little imagination I could have put myself in her place and looked out through her eyes as I remained myself, you see, in my place. And then I could have taken her by the hand and put her in my place so she could look out through my eyes and keep breaking it down all the time until she could see it, and then maybe we could have arrived at a sympathetic understanding of what was involved and a collective decision privately arrived at would have been unanimous. But that would have taken about two hours, and I had only about thirty-five or forty minutes. Now that is why confidence in the integrity of democracy is so hard to maintain.

Now let's jump into another dimension to see exactly what I am talking about because—and bear in mind that the fundamental point that I am making is this—that democracy is grounded in this dynamic, this creative thing that is inherent in life, and therefore it is possible to shape ends—to set up goals, to move toward them, and to bring to bear upon that kind of commitment and conviction the complete resources of one's personality and to hold one's plan or goal at dead center over the raw materials in a chaotic society until, at last, those raw materials begin to take on the objective manifestation of the inner hope.

Now, during times of war, what happens in our own democratic process? We tend to suspend the democratic process in times of social crisis. It is very interesting that we do that. During the Depression in 1932, when Mr. Roosevelt became president of the United States, the banks closed and a lot of other things happened, not because he became president.[7] And Congress did what? We had just moved to Washington;

7. Franklin D. Roosevelt was inaugurated as president on March 4, 1933, amid a rash of bank failures. Two days later, he declared a four-day moratorium on all bank transactions, the so-called bank holiday; and on March 9, only after a few hours of

day after day Congress merely put a rubber stamp on paper after paper that came from the White House. Why? Because everybody was scared to death, and they couldn't risk the democratic process because the time interval that was involved was one that tended to undermine confidence in the integrity of the proposal and the experience itself.

In time of war we did it [again]. We had a man, Jimmy Byrnes, down in South Carolina, who was the czar of something, czar of defense or czar of something—one man; they even dubbed him czar, and nobody thought anything about it because everybody was scared.[8] So that you couldn't trust the [missing word]—time is against you when the emergency is on you unless in your mind there is fixed, in a very definitive and clear-cut and invasive fashion, that time is always on the side of that which has not matured. Now that is the first thing.

Now there is a second thing, and I won't do the second, but the third thing: That democracy is rooted not only in this metaphysical thing about the nature of life and its creative character so that in developing processes and so forth there is always the predisposition on the side that deep within the individuals or deep within the group there is the wisdom which is needful in order that the group might move in the direction that is creative and sound. Now the second thing is what it has to say about the attitude toward people, that human beings are ends in themselves.

I don't know quite how to put this—you remember last Sunday I mentioned the religious insight that man is a child of God. That spelled out in practical terms means that man sees himself as being a person of

---

debate, Congress, bolstered by huge Democratic majorities from the 1932 election, passed the Emergency Banking Relief Act, one of the first pieces of legislation passed during the so-called hundred days, including the Agricultural Adjustment Act (AAA), and creating the National Industrial Recovery Administration (NIRA) and the Tennessee Valley Authority (TVA). Thurman is arguing that despite the large majorities backing President Roosevelt's legislation, the haste with which it was adopted meant that in some ways it was not "democratic."

8. James Byrnes (1892–1972), appointed to the U.S. Supreme Court in 1941, gave up a position as associate justice the following year to head the Office of Economic Stabilization (1942–1943) and Office of War Mobilization (1943–1945), and was widely dubbed the nation's "economic czar." He later served as U.S. secretary of state (1945–1947) and governor of South Carolina (1951–1955), and in the latter position was a vociferous opponent of racial integration.

infinite value. I'd like to pick that idea up and put it here. For all of the insistence in democracy about equality—it has nothing really to do with equality of gifts, with equality of talents, with equality of abilities, with equality even of superficial position, but what fundamentally the genius of democracy insists upon in its notion about equality is this: that the only authentic equality that there is, is the equality of infinite worth. I am not better than you, or you are not better than I am. Those categories mean nothing. But this says that I know that I myself, as far as my little me is concerned, that there is nothing in the heavens above or the earth beneath that can equal what I think my little life is worth to me. I may not be worth anything to you. So, the equality is an equality of quality rather than an equality of quantity. Therefore, it is the insistence, when democracy begins to express itself in behavior patterns, it is the insistence that human beings should never be used as means to other ends: that human beings should never be tails to other kites, but that a human being is an end in himself. That is why, if there is a conflict between human values and property values, democracy insists that human values should take precedence over property values, and on and on we could go.

Therefore, as long as human beings regard themselves as being of infinite worth, however long it may take them to project that sense of infinite value in terms of social forms and political and economic behavior patterns, but as long as men feel that they are of infinite worth, the democratic ideal and dream are a source of inspiration and hope in times when the social processes seem to be out of joint.

Now I'd like to say just one little word about America in this regard. I think often about America, a strange country. But it seems to me, and I hope it will not sound to you as if I am talking on the Fourth of July in some sort of chauvinistic rallying point; but this is a part of the faith, and I would like to take time to say it to you: That I think God through the instrumentality of life and the life process is always at work on the revelation and the demonstration of creative purpose. That is a basic proposition. It is no accident, for instance, that in the period between the eighth century BC and the second century AD every single basic philosophic and ethical insight known to modern man emerged, just in that little period of a thousand years. Every one, all the great religions, all the great ethical insights, the philosophers just in that period between the eighth century BC and about the second century AD.[9] Which seems to suggest, you see, that life was trying to get a backlog of social insight, of ethical and religious insight, as a part of the heritage of the race before the secrets of nature became available to the minds of men. And we are alarmed now because we wonder whether there is enough character in modern man to structure the tremendous power that is his as a result of the way in which he has discovered the secrets of nature. What would be our alarm and amazement if that discovery antedated this thousand years? So I think life is alive with a sense of moral incentive and purpose, and that is an illustration of it.

Now I think that the same thing applies in America. Is it an accident that between these two oceans people from the ends of the earth came in a climate that is ideal for the most part, with natural resources that in some ways seem to be boundless and limitless, and not only that but the one place in which from the beginning of the country itself certain political and ethical ideals were a part of the immediate climate. Isolated, forced to experiment with neighborliness, or not survive. Exposed in the intensity of the isolation to a far-reaching and radical political and ethical theory expressed in the democratic dogma and in the Christian ethic, as if life said, "somewhere on the planet I must set up a laboratory against the time when time and space would be reduced to zero."

Now if time and space are annihilated and men have not had a chance to develop a sense of neighborliness then they will quickly in self-defense destroy each other. But if somewhere on the planet a laboratory can be set up so that men can experiment creatively and effectively in relatedness in neighborliness and so forth, then it may be possible that when time and space are annihilated through the secrets of nature being revealed to the mind of man, that the sense of the family of the human race will step into the vacuum created thereby and make the world a safe and a decent place for all the people who haven't had a chance or time or opportunity

---

9. This simultaneous flowering of transcendental thinking is now often called, following the German philosopher Karl Jaspers (1889–1969), the Axial Age. Jaspers's best-known account, *The Origins and Goal of History* (New Haven, CT: Yale University Press, 1953), was published in English after Thurman's sermon, but the idea precedes the work of Jaspers.

to experiment with neighborliness, probably speaking a language that the rest of us didn't understand.

One generation, two generations, three, four, five removed, that's all . . . somebody who calls attention to the meaning of this so as to keep alive the focal point of the purpose of the impersonal forces of life through which God is operating. Now suppose we knew about atomic energy, and there had been nowhere on this planet—I want you to hear this and think about it, whether you agree or disagree, it doesn't matter—but suppose that all of the development of atomic energy was available to man with the resulting annihilation of time and space, reducing those to zero; suppose all that had taken place on this planet and nowhere on the planet there existed or had existed for any length of time the things we take for granted in American life, what would be the result? Therefore I say to you that I don't think we are in a position of leadership in the world because we are rich or because we have industrial know-how. I think all those are incidental. I will put it that way. But I think that we are in the fateful position of being the only nation on this planet that has had three hundred years of primary exposure to something like the democratic ethic and the Judeo-Christian ethic in an environment so isolated that it could be relatively under control, and with the richest cross section of human beings collected anywhere else in the world. And who are we that such a privilege could be given to us in order that we might strut and throw our weight around to dominate the earth. No, that isn't the meaning of it. The meaning of it is that we have been given this; we have been sent to school by Life, by God, to develop confidence and faith, technique, methodologies for implementing the dream of one world, one family that God has for the human race. And school is out, school is out, and there isn't enough time to do any teaching now.[10] There is just time enough left for contagion. Either we demonstrate or die. There is no alternative left, and I wonder what God thinks about his students. I wonder.

---

10. See the similar use of the metaphor "school's out" in "America in Search of a Soul," printed in the current volume.

A FAITH TO LIVE BY: DEMOCRACY
AND THE INDIVIDUAL II

October 26, 1952
Fellowship Church

In this final sermon in the "Faith to Live By" sermon series, Thurman offers a compelling and creative interpretation of the narrative of Ahab and Naboth.[1] Within the context of growing tensions in Indochina, Thurman argues that balancing equality and freedom is difficult to translate into the spirit of democratic life among the poor and powerless. Addressing the United States' complicity with French colonialism in Asia, he contends that those who are in power are concerned most with "the perpetuation of the established order and therefore live up to the integrity of the power position which is ours to strangle, strangle all of the prerogatives of the Naboth, the little man."

America, because of its position and power in the world, stands where the king stood in the biblical story and therefore bears moral responsibil-

---

1. 1 Kings 21:1–16: The story of Ahab and Naboth's vineyard is a popular text in the Jewish and Christian traditions, depicting a powerful king, Ahab, and his desire to seize the vineyard of a peasant farmer. Ahab was the seventh king of Israel, reigning from ca. 871 to ca. 852 BCE. The Book of Kings depicts him as a weak and frivolous monarch, confronted by Elijah and other prophets, and aided in his cruelty by his powerful queen, Jezebel. Naboth, a Jezreelite, refused Ahab's request because the vineyard was his ancestral inheritance and could not be transferred because by religious law and custom the land ultimately belonged to God. Ahab and Jezebel conspired to take the vineyard through fraudulent claims and had Naboth executed by stoning him to death (vv. 8–16). The biblical story had been used by Sumner Welles (1892–1961), undersecretary of state for President Franklin D. Roosevelt, and a main architect of his "Good Neighbor Policy" with Latin America, to make a similar point about American overreach (Sumner Welles, *Naboth's Vineyard: The Dominican Republic, 1844–1924* [New York: Payson & Clarke, 1928]).

ity for "the little man." "The Naboth dimension of American democracy," according to Thurman, rests upon the doctrine of the infinite worth of the individual and forms the basis for a covenantal relationship between God and the individual that mutually binds the individual and God to a way of life that is expressive of the democratic genius. Two basic affirmations underscore this covenant between the individual and God as they relate to democracy. One is the moral inviolability of the individual, that is, persons must never be used as means to an end. This vertical pole finds its source in the creative intent of God for persons. Speaking of Naboth's refusal to relinquish his vineyard to Ahab, Thurman reflects:

> *This covenant was the basis, the root, the core of the individual's sense of worth. He (Naboth) had a covenant with God. He rated having a covenant with God. This covenant which he had with God was binding upon God as God related to him. This covenant which was the basis of his freedom and the meaning of his life took precedence over any other relationship. If standing within the context of the covenant which he had with God he was required to do anything by any person which did violence to this covenant then he was under moral obligation to defy that power, that force, whoever it was … the covenant with God relates in a moral sense the individual to God and God to the individual.[2]*

The horizontal pole of this relationship between individuality and democracy finds its expression in the related principles of equality and freedom, which likewise have their basis in the infinite worth of the individual. Thurman interprets both principles in light of a theocentric perspective that views the creative intent for community as the normative framework for their meaning and authenticity. In respect to the principle of equality, his definition is illuminative of the covenantal motif mentioned above. He contends that "the only ultimate basis for equality is the equality of infinite worth [of the individual]." Equality, in this sense, goes beyond abilities, qualities, possessions, talents, fate, class, or race. It ascribes supreme worth to the individual as a child of God.

---

2. See p. 88, this volume.

As for Sunday's discussion on democracy, it seems we cannot do two things.[3] First, develop the concept a little further and examine more accurately and perhaps more significantly the timeless foundation on which it rests. I'd like to focus our thought, therefore, on the central aspect of the democratic idea, as it has to do with the respect for the individual. I confess to you that my own mind has been troubled for many years with reference to the basic idea, because I have not been able, as far as my own thinking is concerned, to get to the bottom[4] of this basic thing that I feel so deeply about the meaning of the individual. Of course, you may say at the end of the next thirty minutes or so that once again I am where I started out because the key to the future of man on this planet, I think, is tied up in how one man relates to another man, and what one man means to himself and in the light of that meaning what the other man means to him.

There is a story told in the Old Testament about a king. The king's name was Ahab. Ahab was an oriental despot. He had absolute power over his subjects: he was a ruler with all that that means. The will of the king was not to be questioned. The role of the king among the people was to some extent an absolute role. Now there was a little man in that kingdom who had a vineyard. He had spent much time cultivating that vineyard. It was his vineyard inherited from his father and his father's father and his father's father. Ahab wanted the vineyard so he said, "I want it. If it is necessary, I'll give you something for it. I don't want to steal it." But of course, the king can't steal, he takes. "But we'll work out something." But Naboth said, "I don't want to give it up. It's mine. It's my father's father's father's. This is an extension of myself, and all of the meaning of my little life is wrapped up here in some magical and mysterious manner. My sense of security is here, so you can't have it."

Now get the feeling of this because I want you to hold it in mind as we work this out. The king, the absolute monarch, sees a little patch of land owned by a little man. The king says, "I want it." The little man says, "You can't have it." Can you think of the implications of that? And Ahab

---

3. Thurman seems to lose his train of thought here and never completes the contrast.

4. The opening of the sermon to this point has been transcribed from audio tape.

was powerless to take it apparently. And his wife, Jezebel, helped him work out a scheme, and the rest of the story is full of disaster. And the meaning of the story is that there was something inviolate in the life of the little man that even a king who had absolute power dare not trespass upon. There it is.

Put over against that the significance of the ordinary man in, oh, let us say, in Greek philosophy. And I mention it not for any purposes that may seem to be full of exhibitionism, but the Greeks have influenced us so much and are so wrapped up in almost everything we think that if you took the Greeks out of our civilization, I mean their influence and their ideas, we'd be pretty barren. Of course, we don't have to recognize it as such, but there it is. So, let's look at it for a moment.

You remember *Antigone* last year?[5] When we gave *Antigone* in the arts festival and the role that the Greek chorus played? Now the central figures in the play *Antigone* were kings and queens and blooded stock, as it were—(those whose blood was royal, whatever kind of blood that is—but they were royal)—and they had the center of the stage. All the issues turned on that. They had that—they were involved in the meaningful experiences. And what role did the little man play? What role did the, well the ordinary man, the man in the street as we would say today, just a little man, what role did he play? He was the chorus[6] standing over here, not involved in the traffic, you see, not involved in the meaningful operation. He didn't count, he could only echo something, you see: Mr. and Mrs. Anonymous. But the people who really were it, the king, the queen, the people who rated.

Now we see that same thing reflected in Plato, who has influenced us profoundly. The really significant people are the people within certain classes, the business people, the philosophers, and warriors. But the rank

---

5. The Fellowship Church held its Religious Arts Festival in 1949. It included a production of *Antigone,* written by Sophocles ca. 442 BCE. The festival was intended to demonstrate the "use of drama as a form of worship" (HT, *Footprints of a Dream: The Story of the Church for the Fellowship of All Peoples* [New York: Harper & Brothers, 1959], 93–94).

6. Thurman is referencing the ancient Greek chorus, whose function in plays, especially tragedies, was to perform in the background and dance, recite, and comment on the main events of the performance but never engage in the actual events of the narrative.

and file of the people existed only as they guaranteed the life of this privileged few.[7]

Now Aristotle went even further than that. Aristotle cut out everybody but the philosopher.[8] If you were a warrior, that was all right, but you didn't really count very much unless you were a philosopher. Now if you were a philosopher, then the greatest service which an ordinary man can render life is to keep you going. You know, work for you, take care of you, and sustain you and support you because you were the spearhead of the forward movement of the human race. That is one of the feelings, I imagine.

In Egypt the ordinary man was the dust of the earth. The king was the great . . . When I was in India in Hyderabad, the Nizam of Hyderabad[9] put one of his twenty-five or thirty automobiles at our disposal. And he assigned us a Muslim chauffeur who was to carry us everywhere we went for four days. Every time we came out he was there with the car, waiting to do whatever we wanted. For three and a half days I tried to get some conversation out of this Muslim. He spoke English, but he didn't speak any English to *me*. He was silent, Sphinx-like. The last day when we were being driven to the railway station, I found out the quality of his voice for I heard it for the first time. What did he say as we were riding along, apropos of nothing? "Only God is interested in a poor man." Now he is reflecting this whole thing. Why is this radical difference in the story with which I began in the other recital of the events, that here is an ordinary man who defies the king?

---

7. Thurman was not a fan of Plato (ca. 428–348 BCE) political philosophy, and in a 1958 sermon he compared Plato's *Republic* to *Mein Kampf*; see *PHWT*, 4: 218. A possible source of Thurman's anti-Platonic animus is Karl Popper's *The Open Society and Its Enemies*, 2 vols. (London: Routledge, 1945), the first volume of which was titled *The Spell of Plato*.

8. Although Aristotle (ca. 384–322 BCE) was Plato's pupil, most scholars see his conception of civil society, as outlined in his *Politics*, though justifying slavery and hostile to democracy, as less hierarchical than that of his teacher.

9. Hyderabad was the largest and wealthiest of the princely states, ruled by a Muslim dynasty from the early eighteenth century on. The Nizams of Hyderabad ruled under the British as client monarchs until their powers were ended by an independent India in 1948. The basis of their wealth was the famous Golconda diamond mines, and Osman Ali Khan (1886–1967), the Nizam from 1911 to 1948, was one of the wealthiest persons in the world.

Now let's examine it because the basis of the democratic genius is wrapped up in this explanation, I think. There was an assumption that the individual man had a covenant, an agreement with God, which covenant, which agreement, was binding on him and on God. This covenant stated in the language, that kind of language, this covenant was the basis, the root, the core of the individual's sense of worth. *He* had a covenant with God. He rated having a covenant with God. The covenant which he had with God was binding upon God, as God was related to him. This covenant which was the basis of his freedom and the meaning of his life took precedence over any other relationship. If standing within the context of the covenant which he had with God he was required to do anything by any person that did violence to this covenant, then he was under moral obligation to defy that power, that force, whoever it was. To me that is very amazing, very amazing, very interesting, and very terrifying. Now do you get the picture, that the covenant with God which relates in a moral sense the individual to God and God to the individual? "So even Ahab the king has no right to put any kind of pressure upon me, the little man," said Naboth, "if that pressure does violence to this covenant." Now there it is.

Now it is for this reason, as it would seem to me, that when you say that, logically, the next step (now watch this very carefully) is that all of the people who are related to you in terms of culture, of social pattern, of religion, of national origin and so forth, are therefore, in a way that is unique as far as you are concerned, bound by the same sort of covenant. They are related to the Creator of Life in the same way as you are; therefore they become uniquely related to you. And the things that you are under obligation to do with them, for them, on their behalf, are identical with the things that the covenant dictates to you. Now on that basis what starts out as the genius of democracy in the life of the individual becomes quite consistently in its social implication the basis for a group pride and a group arrogance.

Let me say that again—I feel a vacuum. Let's try it again because I hope I can get it. Now here we are. The individual has the covenant with God. That is the theory and the experience as is seen here in the story of Ahab. And it is this covenant with God that is unique in the sense that it is mine. Now you have one too, but I am not talking about yours.

This is mine. And it binds God morally to me, and it binds me morally to him. On the basis of that covenant the whole pattern of my behavior is dictated and determined. Now when I look at you and I find that you speak the same language as I do, you are part of my same culture, we are all here together, then very quickly I assume that the covenant that binds me in the unique manner binds you, because we are one in all these other ways, you see, language, culture, religion, and so forth. But when I lift up my eyes and see someone way over there who speaks another language, whose culture is different, whose whole orientation is radically different from mine, then it is quite reasonable, is it not, for me to assume that the limitations of the covenant and the ethical implications thereof, are limitations that are bounded by common culture, common language, common religion. So that which starts out in me as the basis for my own self-esteem and self-estimate and moves to you as the basis of your self-esteem and self-estimate, because you and I are of the same language, the same culture, the same background, may become something which is fundamentally divisive; that makes for separateness as I look out upon people whose language, culture, and so on may be different from mine.

So that the problem then in the movement of the democratic experience in the history of mankind has been a problem which has centered around the urgency and the necessity constantly to redefine the boundaries of the group. Because if I do not redefine the boundaries of the group increasingly so as to include more and more diversity, more and more differences, more and more radically alien backgrounds and orientations, then the genius of democracy itself, rooted in this spiritual relationship, becomes a device that makes for group arrogance and group superiority. Do you see what I am talking about? Therefore, the peril of the democratic experience in its very essence is rooted in the fact that the human spirit can never come to a place of rest with reference to the boundaries. Now you can see the kind of conflict that that precipitates in modern life because there are all sorts of other interests that emerge.

Now let me illustrate it if I can. Let us look at the history of our own country in this regard. You will see what I mean. We started out in America in a revolution, you will remember that, that we were born in a revolution, a revolution against a king, against a certain way of life, and so forth, and so on, and on and on it goes. So that there is something in the genius, in the very throb of American life, that relates itself almost instinctively, a sort of collective instinctive feeling to all of the people anywhere in the world who are wrestling with the same thing, who are part of the same respiration that caused us to come to life, whether it is in Asia or Africa or Canada; wherever it is, we respond to the pulse beat of people who are in the throes of the agonies that gave birth to us. That is what I am trying to say. And the meaning then of the democratic notion, experience, insight as far as one aspect of our common life is concerned is to push the boundaries. And we've been responsive in that way.

But along right beside that there has grown up another kind of responsibility: We stand where the king stood. We have position and power in the world we didn't ask for; we have it for all these reasons, some of which I mentioned last Sunday. We are the central or among the central figures on the world stage, and that relationship carries with it its own etiquette and its own morality because it is a position of power and power has its own etiquette, its own morality, its own scale of values; and it may not be at all related to this other thing that gave birth to us and that constantly feeds us and gives us a sense of human dignity and worth and all of those things. So, on the one hand, we feel one with all the people in Indo-China this morning who are in the throes of the kind of agony that gave birth to us.[10] On the other hand, we feel, as a people, under very great obligation to sustain the French government in Indo-China as a part of the etiquette of our position over here in the center of the stage as one of the world powers. So, when we talk about democracy, when we deal with democracy within our common life, our problem is acute because at one time we deal with it as if it were not rooted in this thing about which I

---

10. On September 2, 1945, the Viet Minh, led by Ho Chi Minh, issued the Declaration of Independence of the Democratic Republic of Vietnam. As Thurman perhaps alludes to, its opening sentence copies the famous invocation of inalienable rights in the American Declaration of Independence. The Viet Minh soon found themselves in a war against French colonial forces. By the fall of 1952, the efforts of the French to suppress the independence movement were not going well, and American support for the French efforts was increasing. The French forces withdrew after their defeat at Dien Bien Phu in May 1954. Vietnam was partitioned later that year, and the United States became the main military support for the South Vietnamese government for two decades of bloody warfare. Thurman was a strong anti-imperialist throughout the 1950s; see Eisenstadt, *Against the Hounds of Hell*, 308, 311–12, 465n105.

have been talking for the last twenty-five minutes, but rather that it is rooted in the central, political power arrangement. So, we feel that the only way by which you can hold the established order, the only way by which you can guarantee the perpetuation of the established order and therefore live up to the integrity of the power position which is ours is to strangle, strangle all of the prerogatives of the Naboth, the little man. So, on the one hand, we believe in freedom of speech. That's over here: that's the Naboth dimension of the American democracy, freedom of speech. Over here in the power end of it, if it has bearing on the disturbance of the delicate balance of power in the world, then I'm going to strangle it over here.

Now between those two things you and I move and live and function. So, if I ask you this morning in which one of these dimensions of our relatedness to the democratic dogma you believe, what would you say to me? Would it depend upon what your position in society is? Would it depend upon the degree of your social or economic insecurity or security? Or would you dare let your sense of the meaning of democracy as a basis of your faith in today and tomorrow be rooted in the primacy of the individual's relationship to God and what that relationship in and of itself may lead a man to say and to do?

Now, there is hope as long as men keep alive in themselves the kind of faith about which I have been talking. You may not use the old-fashioned language that you have a covenant with God. I don't care what the language is that you use; every man wants more than anything else in the world to be sure that as a human being he has an importance and a value that is not related to the ups and downs of the standards, the whims, the fears, the anxieties of the society in which he is living. Every man more than anything else in the world wants to know for himself that his significance, his value, is in some wonderfully, mysterious perhaps, but wonderfully exciting manner, more important than anything that he can do, a value that operates at a level in him that cannot be touched by whether he is a good man or a bad man, whether he is evil or righteous, whether he is holy or unholy; every man must know at last that he cannot be destroyed by any of these things. Therefore:[11]

---

11. "Io Victis," in William Wetmore Story, *Poems, Vol. II: Monologues and Lyrics* (Boston: Houghton Mifflin, 1886), 177–79.

I sing the hymn of the conquered, who fell in the Battle of
    Life,—
The hymn of the wounded, the beaten, who died overwhelmed
    in the strife;
Not the jubilant song of the victors, for whom the resounding
    acclaim
Of nations was lifted in chorus, whose brows wore the chaplet
    of fame,
But the hymn of the low and the humble, the weary, the broken
    in heart,
Who strove and who failed, acting bravely a silent and desperate
    part;
Whose youth bore no flower on its branches, whose hopes
    burned in ashes away,
From whose hands slipped the prize they had grasped at, who
    stood at the dying of day
With the wreck of their life all around them, unpitied,
    unheeded, alone,
With Death swooping down o'er their failure, and all but their
    faith overthrown.

And if that is active in you, no tyranny can destroy it, and no madness
in the mind of man can unseat it, for it is God's gift to the human spirit.
And it's so wonderful that it is true.

HUMAN FREEDOM AND
THE EMANCIPATION PROCLAMATION

Pulpit Digest 43
(December 1962): 46–50

*When Howard Thurman was a young boy, growing up in the early years
of the twentieth century, Emancipation Day was celebrated as a holiday by
Black Americans in his hometown of Daytona, Florida, and elsewhere. He
was no doubt present for its celebration in 1913, when, as described in a local
Black newspaper, its highlight was a float with "four old mothers who were
eyewitnesses to the liberating of the race." He would attend two years later
when Emancipation Day was celebrated "in a grand style . . . with a grand
parade, consisting of floats, music, etc."[1]*

*Less than a decade later, in January 1922, Thurman, then a junior at
Morehouse College, delivered an Emancipation Day oration, "Our Challenge." It is the first substantial piece of his writing that survives. It opened,
"Physical slavery is no more," though, he argued, Black Americans were still
bound and victims of what he called "psychic slavery," enslaved to their com-
placency, enslaved by fears of "the white man," to whom too many grant "the
nature of a god."[2] "Our Challenge" is an early and fairly immature work,
and the argument in "Human Freedom and the Emancipation Proclamation" is in many ways very different. But forty years after "Our Challenge,"
Thurman was still asking many of the same questions; what did it mean to*

---

1. See Peter Eisenstadt, *Against the Hounds of Hell: A Life of Howard Thurman*
(Charlottesville: University of Virginia Press, 2021), 25. For a history and anthropol-
ogy of emancipation celebrations, and the many and various dates on which they have
been held, see William H. Wiggins Jr., *O Freedom! Afro American Emancipation
Celebrations* (Knoxville: University of Tennessee Press, 1987).

2. HT, "Our Challenge," in *PHWT*, 1:20–22. For an analysis, see Eisenstadt,
Against the Hounds of Hell, 68–70.

be free, and in particular what did it mean for Black Americans to be free, living in a country that subjected them to various species of unfreedom?

The Emancipation Proclamation, employing the precise, clipped, and legalistic language of a military order, is notoriously unemotional, unlike Lincoln's soaring oratory elsewhere. But "Human Freedom and the Emancipation Proclamation" was not concerned with the specific words or even the complex political circumstances surrounding its issuance. It was rather, as Thurman writes, listening for the "feeling-tone" behind its words. The proclamation irrevocably committed the United States to the abolition of legal slavery, but as Thurman suggested in "Our Challenge," forms of "psychic slavery" and unfreedom did not end in 1865. A slave society for Thurman was the most complete realization of a social order in which a person's worth was solely determined by their position or rank within it, rather than their abilities or their inherent, God-given worth. Emancipation did not abolish this pernicious social ideal or the belief in the necessity of invidious social hierarchies. As Thurman says, "any arrangement in society" that "denies this birthright is not merely amoral, but from within the religious assumption must be regarded as an act against God." But having a sense of one's "infinite worth" is still only freedom as potential.

Thurman goes on to offer two, somewhat different, definitions of freedom. First, freedom is "the capacity to influence critically or determine the future by action in the present." In this view, a free person shapes and is not merely shaped by the social forces about them, and, therefore, rejects the determinism that there are forces over which they have no say nor control. This was precisely the position of the freed people after 1865, aware of the limitations they faced, determined to take full advantage of anything at their disposal to shape their individual and collective futures. And this required a belief that one's destiny, one's history, had not already been predetermined. If the future has already been set, your free will and freedom have been extinguished. "Either life is essentially finished, fixed, set, frozen, or it is essentially fluid, dynamic, creative"; and if you believe the former, "then it is not within the power of the individual to alter any given situation in which he may be involved." In this way, freedom is the belief that, as a free person, you can use your freedom creatively.

Does this imply, asks Thurman, that those with no apparent freedom, such as enslaved persons, are completely without freedom, totally lacking in free will, and that the realities of slavery are radically incommensurate with the experience of freedom? Thurman argues that is not the case, and offers an "enlargement or a tightening of my first working definition of freedom." Freedom now "is the sense of alternatives or options." However dire one's external circumstances, as long as you can imagine or believe in the possibility of an alternative life, your freedom is not entirely extinguished. Enslaved people, he implies, carried this spark of their "infinite worth" in their lives, in their spirituals, and in their religion, passed down from generation to generation. And the lesson was that "the free man, however, with full knowledge of his helplessness to alter the circumstances, can affirm his freedom by determining how he will react to them. This is the mark of his freedom." And this was not a freedom from obligation, but the freedom to take on obligations.³ He was writing this sermon, as he notes, when James Meredith, by entering the University of Mississippi, and Blacks all over the South and the North were trying to realize their freedom by taking responsibility for their individual and collective lives, and for the destiny of America. Or as Thurman had written forty years earlier in "Our Challenge," "we have been freed, now let us be free" for "no one can do it for us!"⁴

January 1, 1963, marks the hundredth anniversary of the issuing of the Emancipation Proclamation by President Abraham Lincoln. It is sobering to reflect that the proclamation gave to the meaning of human freedom a content that was at variance with much of the practice within the several states and the Christian church, for at that fateful moment in our history, several million human beings were precise property and specific chattel.

The feeling-tone of the background against which the new meaning of freedom was expressed in the Emancipation Proclamation can be communicated by an incident from my childhood. I was employed by a family in my hometown in Florida to keep the leaves raked on the lawn during the fall months. In this family there was a little girl who took great

---

3. Thurman likely exaggerates the extent to which "the slave had only a limited responsibility for his own actions"—perhaps, as he suggests, their enslavers saw them as child-like, but it was not how they viewed themselves. However, this does not alter his main argument.

4. HT, "Our Challenge."

delight in following me around in the yard as I raked the leaves in piles. She was interested in the different colors of the leaves. On this particular day, as soon as I had raked the leaves into a pile, she would scatter them again in search of a variety of hues to be found in leaves which from her point of view were at the bottom of the pile. This meant that I would have to do my work over again. Finally I grew exasperated and urged her to stop. She refused. Whereupon I said: "When your father comes home this afternoon, I will report you to him." This was very threatening to her because she stood in great fear of her father. Her reaction to this threat was to reach into her little white pinafore, extract a straight pin, run over to me, and jab it into my hand. I reacted quite naturally by exclaiming: "Have you lost your mind?" In utter amazement she said: "That didn't hurt you! You can't feel!"[5]

The Emancipation Proclamation announced that the slaves were human beings and, as such, not only were free intrinsically as children of God, but also that no human agency had the right to abrogate that freedom by holding them in bondage. Whatever may have been the economic basis of slavery, the moral issue was clear. In this instance, the president of the United States, acting on behalf of the State, took a position in keeping with the ethical genius of the Judeo-Christian tradition, while the several states which held slaves and the Christian churches which supported them stood squarely against the ethical insight. It is this moral conflict that was at once the metaphysical and religious issue that resulted in the Civil War. After one hundred years, this fundamental issue remains undecided. In one form or another, it still stands before the American conscience. The terrible and heart-rendering recent spectacle at Oxford, Mississippi, is but a grim reminder of the fact that the issue has not been decided.[6]

---

5. This story is told, with a male protagonist, in the introduction to the present volume.

6. The effort of James Meredith (b. 1933) in the fall of 1962 to become the first Black student to enroll at the University of Mississippi in Oxford was blocked by the segregationist governor Ross Barnett (1898–1987). Because of Barnett's recalcitrance, President Kennedy assigned federal marshals to assist Meredith's registration, and activated federal troops and federalized the Mississippi National Guard. On the evening of September 30, a violent riot by armed segregationists left two dead and injured several hundred persons. Order was restored by some 25,000 federal troops

It is important that thoughtful consideration be given to the significance of human freedom against the background of the Emancipation Proclamation in the centennial year of its celebration. One of the great religious beliefs upon which Western civilization rests is that the human soul is of infinite and intrinsic worth before God. This is a radical affirmation because it insists that the worth of the individual does not rise from social classification, economic condition, or confession of faith, but is a part of the "givenness" of God, inherent in the fact of the existence of the individual. Freedom must be thought of initially as the birthright of the individual human being. Any arrangement in society, of whatever kind, growing out of any ascribed necessity that denies this birthright is not merely amoral but from within the religious assumption must be regarded as an *act against God*.

I begin therefore with my first working definition. Freedom is the capacity to influence critically or determine the future by action in the present. The first word of emphasis here is capacity. The capacity is potential in the individual. The actualizing of this potential is the individual's experience of freedom. During the period of childhood and innocence, this capacity is relatively inactive and of a very limited kind because of the absence of formal responsibility. It is a commonplace thing to say that there is a kind of freedom of innocence. In the life of the child this is very important because it means that the organism is deeply engaged in establishing itself in laying the physiological and neurological track upon which the adult individual will move. If the child is forced to cope with his environment prematurely and thereby deal with his environment as if he were an adult, then this important process is interrupted. The nervous system becomes angry, and anti-social behavior patterns develop, and the environment becomes the enemy. There is no more important function of society than the building of windbreaks behind which children may be *children*. The kind of freedom that belongs to innocence is an essential prelude to the freedom that goes with responsibility. One of the most horrendous evils of human slavery was the terrible effect that it had on

---

and National Guardsmen, one of the largest massing of military personnel for a domestic disturbance in American history. Meredith registered on October 1, and the Oxford riot is seen as a turning point in the Kennedy administration's and the federal government's active support and intervention on behalf of Black civil rights.

the children of the slaves. Almost from birth, they had to grapple with their environment with the presumption of maturity.

I remember one day visiting an apple orchard in the West. The owner was selling from a roadside stand. It happened that these were apples that could not be marketed even though they were firm and delectable. However, each one had one or two places in which the skin was hard and the flesh underneath the marks was dry and lifeless. I asked what had happened to produce this condition. I was told that, when the apples were very young, and had just begun to grow, a hailstorm came, and these were the bruised spots. The growth of the apples was not completely hindered, but the bruised places died.[7]

The second word of emphasis in my initial working definition is "determine." The meaning of the term is to shape, to alter, to mold, to fashion.

This suggests something very important about the nature of life. Either life is essentially finished, fixed, set, frozen, or it is essentially fluid, dynamic, creative.

If the former is the case, then it is not within the power of the individual to alter any given situation in which he may be involved. To state it categorically, there isn't anything that anybody can do to alter anything. If such is a man's assessment of life, he is in a favorable position if life is set or fixed advantageously for him: there would be no necessity for him to want to change anything. It would also be to his benefit if those persons in his society who were not advantaged accepted the fact of the hard-fixed patterns. Seen from this vantage point, any effort on the part of the disadvantaged to alter the situation is regarded as an act of rebellion against life. And if a theological reference is used, it is regarded as an act of rebellion against God. Under such circumstances, an individual who acts as if he has the capacity to determine the future by action in the present may very easily be called Antichrist. Such a reference was used in a television statement in connection with the tragedy in Oxford, Mississippi. Responsibility for the "shape of things to come" must rest signifi-

---

7. Thurman uses the analogy of the bruised apple in "What Can I Believe In?" *The Journal of Religion and Health* 12 (November 1972): 111–19.

cantly, though not totally, upon the shoulders of the individuals who are functioning in the present.[8]

This leads me directly into an enlargement or a tightening of my first working definition of freedom.

Freedom is the sense of alternatives or options. The essential word here is "sense"; for it is the sense of alternative that guarantees the freedom. It may be literally true that the individual in any given circumstance may be unable to implement an alternative. He may be victimized by forces over which he is unable to exercise any control whatsoever. There may be circumstances that are not to his will, however determined or righteous his will may be. He may be held in the agonizing grapple of the elements in his situation that for the extent or duration of his life will remain unchanged and unaltered. But as long as he has a sense of option, he is free. It is for this reason that groups which have been held in bondage, generation after generation, without yielding the nerve center of their consent to the bondage, have, in ways that can be understood and in ways that transcend the furthest rim of rational reflection, kept alive the active dream of freedom.

One very cold winter day in January, I was riding along the lake shore in Milwaukee when I noticed at a point near the beach dozens of ducks and other fowl disporting themselves in the water even though the lake as far as the eye could see was frozen. My friend stopped his car so that I could go over and take a look. I discovered that, through a pipe that opened on the surface of the lake, a constant stream of hot water was flowing. This made it impossible for the water to freeze around that area, even though the temperature was below zero and the lake itself was frozen. This is what the sense of alternative does in the life of the individual who is held in a situation in which it is impossible for him in any given time element to influence or alter.[9]

---

8. Taken from the title of a science-fiction novel by H. G. Wells, *The Shape of Things to Come* (New York: Macmillan, 1933).

9. Thurman, in a sermon from the previous year, said that he had recently been in Milwaukee, and the warm water pipe into Lake Michigan was the gift of a wealthy benefactor who did not want to see birds freeze in the cold Wisconsin winters (HT, "The Inner Light I," October 22, 1961), HTC. Thurman's visit probably occurred in March 1959, when he had an engagement at the congregation of his good friend Rabbi Dudley Weinberg. In his 1961 sermon, Thurman said the fountain demonstrates that

When there is no sense of alternative, there is no active ability or concern for determining the future by any kind of action in the present. The condition in the present is coextensive with the future, and the basis of hope and the grounds of freedom disintegrate.

One of the most striking sermons that I heard as a boy in my home town was preached by a visiting evangelist. It was a sermon on hell. He told a story in the first person to the effect that he had visited hell and was given a personally conducted tour. The people whom he saw in hell were there because they had been guilty of two sins in particular—dancing and card playing. The first place to which he was taken was a vast dancing hall. In this dancing hall, millions of couples were dancing. They had to dance forever—and with the same partners. They could neither stop nor rest. The next place was a huge room with thousands of tables. At each one four people were seated playing cards. They had to play cards throughout eternity without stopping. The deeds that had caused them to go to hell, they had to do forever. There was no burning lake, no fire, no devil. The thing that made it hell was the fact that they had no alternatives. All options were frozen. The one critical thing, the precious ingredient in human life, was gone—freedom, the sense of alternative and option.

There is a definite responsibility that is the concomitant of freedom. First, there is the responsibility for one's own actions. This kind of responsibility is implicit in my working definition of freedom, for, if freedom is the capacity to act in the present so as to influence or determine the future, to that extent is the future for the individual geared to his personal action. It is obvious that this has limitations, but the basic idea is valid. The Emancipation Proclamation made manifest this kind of responsibility. The slave had only a limited responsibility for his own actions, and the limitation was in the hands of the slave owner. The slave as such could not presume to have responsibility for his own actions except in terms of the slave-system. He was under no necessity to have any sense of the future or any responsibility for it. He was a kept, not a maintained, human being. With the coming of the Emancipation Proclamation, the slave was faced with the responsibility of his future. The symbol of freedom in a society is social accountability. Here is one of the strange para-

"nothing is ever quite frozen over," and that "there is a fluid center in man in which he may discover clues to the meaning of life about him."

doxes of freedom as made manifest in the Emancipation Proclamation. The freed slave became socially responsible for his actions; the freed slave had a negligible social experience in this kind of accountability. This lack became one of the strong arguments for the condemnation of the Proclamation itself. The polite form of the paradox is the statement: the Negro is a child. The most devastating expression of the contradiction is found, primarily in the former slave-holding states, in the common reference to a Negro of whatever age (ten or ninety) as "boy." The far-reaching effect of the Emancipation Proclamation all over the world is the announcement that human dignity requires social accountability.

A second kind of responsibility, growing out of freedom, is for one's personal reaction to the experience of life. This is more hazardous than what is involved in social accountability. To be responsible for one's reaction to the events of one's life is the high mark of human freedom.

It is true that the solitary individual may be unable to determine the nature and the character of the events that he encounters in his living. There may sweep in upon him forces that in no sense take him into account. Again and again, a man's life may be buffeted by experiences that seem blind and reckless, and utterly impersonal in their cruelty.

The free man, however, with full knowledge of his helplessness to alter the circumstances, can affirm his freedom by determining *how* he will react to them. This is the mark of his freedom.

The Emancipation Proclamation affirms that every man has this capacity. Ultimately, this is the meaning of the creative, ethical insight growing out of our faith in its insistence that we are, all of us, children of God. To become like him is to confirm the insight that we are of infinite worth before him. What is the "given" in human beings is also the crown that God holds over us all that from generation unto generation we must grow tall enough to wear.[10]

---

10. For this familiar catchphrase of Thurman, see Eisenstadt, *Against the Hounds of Hell*, 96.

BLACK PENTECOST: FOOTPRINTS
OF THE DISINHERITED

May 31, 1972
Eliot Congregational Church
Roxbury, Massachusetts

For Howard Thurman, the nationalist turn in Black politics, culture, and religion was a challenge, one that left him both wary and encouraged. In some of his writings, most notably in the concluding pages of The Search for Common Ground *(1971), he is outspoken in his condemnation of those who, in his opinion, had made vulgarity into a "trademark" of their liberation from the "contamination of the white society," while dismissing those who disagreed with them as so many "Uncle Toms."[1] But if he was always harshly critical of proponents of racial separation, he was intrigued by the outpouring of enthusiasm for the forms of Black expression and felt a need to understand it, to connect to it, and make a bridge between his own thinking and that of the rising generation. He remained on good terms with and was an inspiration to some of the leading proponents of the new currents of Black political thought, such as Derrick Bell Jr., Lerone Bennett Jr., and Vincent Harding.[2]*

In a 1971 review of J. Deotis Roberts's Liberation and Reconciliation: A Black Theology, *Thurman wrote of being "in the midst of torrents of rhet-*

---

1. HT, *The Search for Common Ground* (New York: Harper & Row, 1971), 97–98.

2. For Thurman's interactions with Black radicalism and nationalism in the 1960s and 1970s, see Peter Eisenstadt, *Against the Hounds of Hell: A Life of Howard Thurman* (Charlottesville, VA: University of Virginia Press, 2021), 368–74; and Peter Eisenstadt, "Three Historians and a Theologian: Howard Thurman's Impact on the Writing of African American History," in *Reconstruction at 150: Reassessing the Revolutionary "New Birth of Freedom,"* ed. Vernon Burton and Brent Morris (Charlottesville, VA: University of Virginia Press, forthcoming).

oric concerning the Black Experience by a wide range of involved and unin-
volved people in society," much of which Thurman found to be overheated
and ill-considered.³ Nonetheless, "the central problem of Black Theology is
not unlike the central issue of any theology—the totality of life grounded in a
spiritual reality which not only bottoms existence but also, at the same time,
infuses and informs life with a divine dimension? More directly, are the God
of life and the God of religion one and the same? If they are, then the Black
Experience cannot be separated from the totality of experience, and the sense
of being cut off or isolated, despite the intensity of the reality, has no ultimate
significance and justification." In the review, Thurman concludes that "rac-
ism is sin, it is evil, it is against God and, therefore, against life . . . and the
basic insistence remains that injustice and hatred between black and white
are evil because they are against life." This was Thurman's Black theology.⁴

---

3. HT, Review of J. Deotis Roberts, *Liberation and Reconciliation: A Black Theology* (Philadelphia: Westminster Press, 1971), in Box 7, Folder 56, HTC. Deotis Roberts (b. 1927) is the author of many books on theology and Black theology. He was president of the Interdenominational Theological Center in Atlanta from 1980 to 1983. It is not clear if Thurman's review was ever published. Both men admired each other. In 1970 Roberts wrote that as a mystic, "Howard Thurman has no rival and no second among his black brothers. It is surprising to me that he has been ignored almost completely in anthologies and works on mysticism. He is, indeed, one of the great mystics of all time. His mysticism is not 'introverted,' nor is it a mysticism of withdrawal from human problems. His mysticism is practical and urges us toward involvement and engagement in the real world where social and ethical issues are at stake"; J. Deotis Roberts, "The American Negro's Contribution to Religious Thought," in *The Negro Impact on Western Civilization*, ed. John Slabey Roucek and Thomas Kiernan (New York: Philosophical Library, 1970), 87.

4. For further comments on Thurman and Black theology see Luther E. Smith, "Black Theology and Religious Experience," in *Journal of the Interdenominational Theology Center* 8, no. 1 (Fall 1980): 59–72; James H. Cone, "The Contradictions of Life Are Not Final: Howard Thurman and the Quest for Freedom," in *The Human Search: Howard Thurman and the Quest for Freedom: Proceedings of the Second Annual Thurman Convocation*, ed. Mozella G. Mitchell (New York: Peter Lang, International Academic Publishers, 1992), 13–25; Walter E. Fluker, "Dangerous Memories and Redemptive Possibilities: Reflections on the Life and Work of Howard Thurman," *Critical Review of International Social and Political Philosophy* 7, no. 4 (January 2004): 147–76; Anthony Sean Neal, *Common Ground: A Comparison of the Ideas of Consciousness in the Writings of Howard W. Thurman and Huey P. Newton* (Trenton, NJ: Africa World Press, 2015); Anthony Sean Neal, *Howard Thurman's Philosophical Mysticism: Love against Fragmentation* (Lanham, MD: Lexington Books, 2019);

In May 1972, making one of his few returns to Boston since leaving Boston University, Thurman delivered three sermons on the assigned topic, Black Pentecost, at the Eliot Congregational Church, a Black church in Roxbury.⁵ After the second sermon, in a question-and-answer session, Thurman provided the following response to the following question: "I am personally disturbed about the emphasis on Blackness today, how it takes on wings ... When the spirit comes, how does that relate to Blackness, as an individual?"

> *I think the important thing that happens is this, that the spirit helps me to put at the disposal of God my experience of life, and the things in my experience that are unique become available to me as a part of that through which the spirit of God in me will speak so that I become more myself, my voice becomes more authentic, and it is not a voice that calls attention to the uniqueness of my experience, it is a voice that calls attention to the fruits of that uniqueness, in my life. I feel very deeply the implications of your comment, and I don't want to get going on that, because we will be here longer than your schedule permits, but an absolute is an absolute, and it is the nature of an absolute to be an absolute, and I have a built-in allergy to any social absolute, because it is the absolute in white society that has lacerated me, and the only thing an absolute knows what to do is to absolute. It doesn't know if it is in the hands of a green man, a yellow man, a Black man, or a white man. I don't like absolutes. He's very jealous, and I'm not about to have him put his thumbs down on me, because the agony of my cry, due to the lacerations of the absolutes in my environment, so I feel it is important in my religious experience to be blessed that through my life as I have lived it, in my journey, in my society, placed in my hands by Him as a sacrament, and to [stop] that possession from reproducing in my experience, internalizing,*

Corey D. B. Walker, "Love, Blackness, Imagination: Howard Thurman's Vision of Communitas," *South Atlantic Quarterly* 112, no. 4 (October 1, 2013): 641–55.

5. For more on the background to Thurman's 1972 sermon series on Black Pentecost, see *PHWT*, 5: 225–33. For his first two appearances at the Black Pentecost event, see the sermon "The Release of the Spirit" and the interview "Reflections on the Black Experience," in the Howard Thurman Virtual Listening Room, at http://archives.bu.edu/web/howard-thurman/virtual-listening-room.

the absoluteness [by which] I have been hammered, so that I match
an absolute with an absolute.

Now that may seem very vague, but that is all I can do now; I can
spell it out, but I feel, you see, that if God speaks to me, he speaks to
me through my idiom, which has nothing to say about yours, except
that if I respond to him out of my idiom and you respond to God out
of your idiom, then the idioms will recognize the voice of God, and I
think that one of the reasons why, instinctively, in our society, walls
have been built up between peoples, trying to keep the idioms apart,
so that the idioms can't talk to each other, because when the idioms
start speaking, then my little plan, and my little limitations and
prejudices [unintelligible]. So I am all for letting God speak through
that which he has been saying through my story, and to hear that,
and in hearing that, to make my ears sensitive to your story.

These themes carried over to the final sermon in the Pentecost series,
"Footprints of the Disinherited." In this sermon Thurman discusses the
Pentecost event itself, arguing that its meaning is that everyone hears "the
Word" in terms of their own life experiences, their own "idiom." He then
speaks specifically of African American Christianity and the experiences of
his grandmother in slavery and freedom, and how Black Christianity could
provide a ground of possibility in situations that were objectively without
hope, and how her spirit and those like her infused Martin Luther King
Jr.'s campaign against Black fear. Thurman concludes by strongly opposing
both religious and racial parochialism: "We cannot have an exclusive notion
of how God works just with us and expect that little notion that we have
to be able to support us as we undertake to include the whole world as our
brothers."

For there is not a word in my tongue, but, lo, O Lord, thou
    knowest it altogether.
Thou hast beset me behind and before, and laid thy hand upon
    me.
Such knowledge is too wonderful for me; it is high, I cannot
    attain unto it.

> Whither shall I go from thy spirit? or whither shall I flee from
>   thy presence?
> If I ascend up into heaven, thou art there: if I make my bed in
>   hell, behold, thou art there.
> If I take the wings of the morning, and dwell in the uttermost
>   parts of the sea;
> Even there shall thy hand lead me, and thy right hand shall steady
>   me.
> How precious also are thy thoughts unto me, O God, God, God!
>   How great is the sum of them!
> If I should count them, they are more in number than the sand:
>   when I awake, I am still with thee.
> Search me, O God, and know my heart: try me, and know my
>   thoughts:
> And see if there be any wicked way in me, and lead me in the way
>   everlasting.[6] Amen.

I shall not trust myself to make any preliminary statement either of appreciation or anything of that sort because it would be grossly inappropriate. All that I can say is that I am greatly privileged to be here tonight, and I want to go at once to that which is on my mind and in my heart to share.

I want to read two things and then take a few minutes to share with you a part of the concern that's in my spirit.

> I dreamt God took my soul to hell. To my right among the trees
> were men working. And I said to God, "I should like to go and
> work with those men. Hell must be a very fruitful place because
> the grass is so green." And God said, "Nothing grows in the gar-
> den they're making." We stood looking, and I saw them work-
> ing among the bushes, digging holes, but in the holes they set
> nothing. And when they had covered them with sticks and earth,
> each man went a way off and set behind the bushes, watching.
> And I noticed that as each walked, he set his foot down care-

---

6. Psalm 139:4–10, 17–18, 23–24 (KJV). This was Thurman's favorite psalm.

fully, looking where he stepped. And I said to God, "Why are they doing that? And what are they doing?" And God said, "They are making pitfalls into which their fellows may sink." And I said to God, "Why do they do that?" And God said, "Because each man thinks that when his brother falls, he will rise." And I said to God, "How will he rise?" And God said, "He will not rise." And I saw their eyes gleam from behind the bushes. And I said to God, "Are these men sane?" And God said, "No, they are not sane. There is no sane man in hell."[7]

"I have never caused anyone to weep," says the Egyptian Book of the Dead.[8] "I have never spoken with a haughty voice. I've never made anyone afraid. I've never been deaf to words of justice and truth."

The most interesting thing about the Day of Pentecost as it is found in the Book is this. The Book lists a large number of people from all over the known world—all the races and cultures; they were there; and the Book names them; you can read it in Acts.[9] And then it goes on to say that they had at Pentecost, that day or evening, an experience unique in their lives; for every man heard the Word in his own tongue. Every man, whether he spoke Greek or—whatever the others are I've forgotten. He heard the Word in his own tongue, and perhaps this is the only way that any man ever hears the Word. For if he is to understand the Word that is said, it has to be in his own tongue. Whatever he may think of his tongue—he may not like his language, he may feel ashamed of it, but if he hears the Word, that's how he hears it. So that a man, then, brings *his* life and *his* experience to the hearing of the Word.

---

7. Olive Schreiner, "The Sunlight Lay across My Bed—," in HT, ed., *A Track to the Water's Edge: The Olive Schreiner Reader* (New York: Harper & Row, 1978), 64, 65–66.

8. The probable source for Thurman's quotation is Emma Craufurd's translation of Simone Weil's *Waiting for God* (1951; repr., New York: Routledge, 2010), 51, where the same text appears in a passage Weil attributes to the Egyptian Book of the Dead.

9. The Book of Acts describes the crowd gathered for the Pentecost event as consisting "of devout Jews from every nation under heaven living in Jerusalem," later listing their nations of origin (Acts 2:5, 9–10).

So when I see in the subject, in the title, that is given me, "Black Pentecost," this is what I interpret it to mean—that the man who has had his unique experience living in his situation in his world at the time interval of his life, whatever word he hears, he hears it through that kind of experience. So it could be green experience, it could be red experience, it could be white experience, it could be black experience; but we're talking about black experience. But the important thing to remember—and I don't want to take too much time on it because I want to get to what's more fundamental in my thought—the thing to remember is that the only life you have is your life; and if you do not live your life, following the grain in your wood, being true to the secret which is your secret, then you must stretch yourself out of shape in order to hear the Word, and this means, you see, that you cannot come to yourself in the Word.

Now that's Part 1.

Now I want to go on to Part 2.

The miracle of God to me is how he is able to give to a man's life that is even in his own estimation worthless a meaning. I will have to draw on my own experience tonight, my own story, and there are two that I want to establish as a setting for what I have to say.

One has to do with my grandmother.[10] How a slave survived, not his body, but how a slave survived with his soul. We are so far removed from it—and I don't want to dwell on it because I don't want you to have nightmares. But we have no sense, no awareness, of what it meant to be a slave, to have no intrinsic worth, to be a thing, sold, exchanged; to have no say over your own body. Now, my grandmother, whenever she saw that the oil was getting low in the lamp—my lamp or my sister's lamp—she would tell us a story from her past, and I want to tell it to you. She was a young woman about twenty-five years old when the Civil War was fought. She was a slave on a plantation in north Florida, just outside of Tallahassee, Florida, in a place called Moseley Hall. Twice a year, the slave owner,[11] together with some of the owners of plantations that neighbored his, would permit a slave who was called of God to preach, to preach to

---

10. For Nancy Ambrose (ca. 1842–ca. 1930), see *PHWT*, 1: xxxi–xxxiii; and Eisenstadt, *Against the Hounds of Hell*, 27–29, 37–38, 43–44.

11. For enslaver John McGehee (1802–1882), see Eisenstadt, *Against the Hounds of Hell*, 28–29.

the slaves. Now, this didn't happen too often, but it did happen. And my grandmother told us that it didn't matter what the subject was about which he was preaching, he always ended his sermons in the same way. Now, some of you are familiar with what that says for the habit of ending your sermon on Calvary, you know. It doesn't matter where you start, you finally end there, you know. It's a part of a kind of idiom.

So he would always end his sermons with this picture. She said he would stand full length and say with his voice to them, "You are not niggers, you are not slaves." And then he would pause, and I can hear her say now, "His eyes would crawl around on all our faces and then he would say, 'You are God's children.'"[12] Now, this sounds so simple and almost so naïve now, but can you imagine what happened to a slave who suddenly felt that despite his place or lack of place in his world, that he was God's child. Now, we have forgotten this. We have forgotten that the only true basis for a sense of security—and I know how this may sound to you—is the awareness that you are precious in the sight of God, that you are of worth, and that your worth is not derived from anything that you do, anything that you have, anything that you know; it is a part of the givenness of God in his children. And you know, if you are anchored there, you lose your fear of life and you lose your fear of people, but most importantly—and I want to dwell here for a minute—most importantly, you lose your fear of death. For you see, as long as a man feels that his physical life is of supreme importance and significance, so long as he places a maximum emphasis on staying alive, if anybody wishes to control him, all he needs to do is to threaten to kill him. But if I have lost my fear of death, it is then that I'm ready to live.

Now this is the contribution that the religion of Jesus makes to mankind. Do you believe that?

One of the insights that's most often overlooked in all of the wonderful things that we say on occasions like this, or other occasions, about Martin King, is this, that the miracle of Martin King, as seen through

---

12. Thurman told this story often, as in *Jesus and the Disinherited* (New York: Abingdon-Cokesbury, 1949), 50. For Martin Luther King Jr.'s use of this story in a student paper, see *PHWT*, 3: xxxix; Quinton Dixie and Peter Eisenstadt, *Visions of a Better World: Howard Thurman's Pilgrimage to India and the Origins of African American Nonviolence* (Boston: Beacon Press, 2011), 190–92.

my particular eyes, was the fact that he was able to inspire in people whose whole lives had been conditioned by fear, to inspire a kind of inner freedom, which made it possible—and so far away as we are from Alabama—but which made it possible for him to inspire an amazing miracle. When you think that for many years, certainly since the last decade of the nineteenth century when the whole pattern of life began to shift in the South for a lot of reasons,[13] that all through that long period, the people to whom he addressed his words and of whom he was one had lived in a climate of fear. Now, please hear the words. They had lived in a climate of fear, and their nervous systems had been conditioned to fear, so that automatically they would not in a moment of a lapse of memory do something that would bring down on their heads the judgment and the violence by which they were surrounded. Now, so that it didn't matter what the excitement was, what the pressure, until Martin King did what I am saying that he did through this grace of God, no child or man or woman in Montgomery would even by accident, because he had a slip of memory, sit up front. There was a built-in mechanism, through years of conditioning, which operated always as an effort to guarantee the continuity of the physical life of the people who live there. Now, the miracle is that when Martin King, not in the name of democracy, not in the name of Americanism, not in the name of even righteousness, but in the name of God, and for the first time at the very core of Protestant orthodoxy in the South, here was an ethical imperative. So that, to reject the imperative in that area of the Bible Belt would be equivalent to rejecting Jesus Christ. So they were in a bind, and it freed these children, and these people, because there was in them now a sense of the operating of the givenness of God. Now, I believe this, and I feel, you see, that all of the ideologies, all the dogmas, all the slogans, will pass, and only the living God will remain.

---

13. Thurman was probably referring to the analysis in C. Vann Woodward's *The Strange Career of Jim Crow* (New York: Oxford University Press, 1955). For more recent accounts, see Orville Vernon Burton, *The Age of Lincoln* (New York: Hill & Wang, 2007), 271–322; and Orville Vernon Burton and Armand Derfner, *Justice Deferred: Race and the Supreme Court* (Cambridge, MA: Harvard University Press, 2021), 84–11.

Now, one more tiny step and the time that I've given to myself will be up, but you don't know what that time is!

We have been for a long time in American Christianity, we have been worshipers of two gods, the God of life—the God of the marketplace, the God of the traffic of existence— and the God of religion.[14] And in a very awkward way we have felt that the God of life always had the advantage of the God of religion. Have you ever said: This is a very wonderful thing to do; it's right, it's decent, it's whatever else that's positive and good about it; but it just is not strategic. It just isn't practical, because the God of the whisper in the heart, by our practice, is not supposed to operate except in the holy place. Now, the miracle of Jesus, the *miracle* of Jesus, is to me that he did not divide his sense of his Father. You see, as the sparrow falls, the hairs of your head are numbered; he is Father, he is Creator, he is Friend. And therefore, if you want to separate yourself from God, then deny the God in you and deny, at the same time, the God in life or in your fellows. Now this, to me, is very interesting, because he, Jesus, took the most intimate, the most exclusive word having to do with that primary blood relationship, "brother," and so filled it with a content that it transcended all the barriers. Now, if he had said, if he had taken the word "cousin," or "uncle," or—no, he took the word that is at the very center of man's exclusive experience—my "brother"—and he poured into that word a meaning that made it universal.[15] And the church has forgotten to remember that, for it says, you see—and I am stopping now, hopefully—it says, you see, that it is possible, and think with me right here, please, it says that it is possible for a sectarian, a parochial religious experience; it's possible for that kind of experience to supply enough energy to support a universal morality, a universal brotherhood.

Now what am I talking about? This is what I am saying, that we cannot have an exclusive notion of how God works just with us and expect that little notion that we have to be able to support us as we undertake

---

14. Thurman often spoke of the artificiality of the distinction between the "God of life" and the "God of religion"; see, for instance, "The Perils of Immature Piety," in *PHWT,* 1: 51; "The Inner Life and World-Mindedness" (1945) and "God and the Race Question" (1946), in *PHWT,* 3: 108–13, 186–90.

15. The Greek word *adelphos* is often used in the New Testament to mean "brethren."

to include the whole world as our brothers. So it means that all the time we've got to keep broadening, widening our religious experience in order that we might be able to support brotherhood as defined in this new and tremendous way of the Master. And this is why he talks so much about love; and for the disinherited, love is something that initially is practiced in the tiny cell in which, in their society, they have been imprisoned.

When my father died when I was seven, and in our neighborhood there was a community, a communion.[16] And we didn't have enough money to buy the coffin, so my mother just said, "Howard, go to the neighbors—we only needed $41.00—go to the neighbors and they will give it." And then when some other neighbor died if they didn't have enough money, my mother gave. You lived in a tight circle in which your own sense of community was your bulwark against the world. Now, what the Master says is, take what you have been learning in that primary experience and carry it to the ends of the earth, and if you can't do it, the experience itself will begin to die. So I must love or perish. And the place where the disinherited learns this is in the primary circle in which their life is cast when all for one and one for all, but without a religious reference, and then suddenly when the insight begins to break upon them, they find that what they have been in school learning to do is *the* lesson.

One more window,[17] and I take the books in my hand.

When I grew up, in our community, it did not ever occur to me that my religious experience, my religious practice, extended beyond the Negro community in which I lived. It just did not ever cross my mind, and a white boy in my town, my age, growing up in the Baptist church or Methodist church downtown, felt the same way about me. The magnetic field of awareness[18] simply stopped at the boundary of my little community. So when I went to seminary, and for the first time in my life I found myself living in a community that was made up of people who were not like me, I had the most horrendous and lacerating experience of my total

---

16. See *WHAH*, 5–6.

17. "Window" is a term Thurman often used to refer to an addition portion of a sermon, a way of seeing something new, a portal to insight and knowledge. See also p. 23.

18. For an earlier account of the "magnetic field of awareness," see HT, *The Luminous Darkness* (New York: Harper & Row, 1965), 3.

life—nothing has touched it since quite like it—trying to broaden the magnetic field of my Christian morality to include my classmates who were not like me. Now, if I could not do this, then the meaning of my faith would disintegrate, so I learned how to keep broadening the field. I'd learned a little about it, because there were some people in my community that I couldn't stand, so they were outside, but I felt under some obligation sometime to get to them.

Now it seems to me that this is, in essence, what the Pentecost message is, the spirit that comes to you in which you hear your own name called. That spirit you must carry wherever you go, doing whatever you are doing. For if you do not, then the spirit in you withers, and very, very quietly your heart will rot, rot, and God will be so sad that he permitted you to be born.

America in Search of a Soul

January 20, 1976
University of Redlands
Redlands, California

*"America in Search of a Soul" was delivered in the year of the bicenten-
nial celebration of the United States as the Omar Robbins Lecture in Religious Studies for 1976 at the University of Redlands.[1] Thurman was also
awarded an honorary Doctor of Divinity degree on that occasion. Composed
during the infamous 1975–1976 Boston busing crisis,[2] Thurman's concern
with events in Boston is reflected here, especially in the way he uses such
terms as "schools" and "neighborhoods" as spiritual metaphors. This lecture
underscores Thurman's concern with racism as an obstacle to Americans'
realization of democracy at home and in the world and captures the essence
of Thurman's understanding of the American democratic experiment in
world history, and what he perceives as a divine initiative to test the will and
potential of human freedom and responsibility in creating what he called
"the search for common ground."*

*"The American Dream," says Thurman, "... is a dream of equality, of
justice, [and] freedom." While this hackneyed expression, in many ways, has
become a staple of American democratic discourse, taken in the context of*

---

1. "America in Search of a Soul" was published originally in Walter Earl Fluker
and Cathy Tumber, eds., *A Strange Freedom: The Best of Howard Thurman on Religious
Life and Public Experience* (Boston: Beacon Press, 1998), 265–71. The lecture has
been transcribed from audiotape for reproduction here, giving readers some sense of
Thurman's extemporaneous speaking style. However, the editors have not included his
opening reading of the Gettysburg Address.

2. Thurman had provided pastoral counsel to one of the families featured in
J. Anthony Lukas's definitive account of this painful episode in *Common Ground*
(New York: Vintage Press, 1986), as he had with so many others—Black and white—
struggling with racial injustice.

the late 1970s and his broader perspective on community, it provides a useful key to Thurman's vision of the inherent challenges and contradictions of creating and fostering a national community. His concern was rooted in the contraction of what he called "neighborliness," the relational and structural restrictions on democratic rights and responsibilities of minoritized populations within the United States. "Neighborliness" represents the inner dispositions and attitudes necessary for creating democratic space in "a friendly world under friendly skies."[3]

Howard Thurman's interpretation of the just society, implied in the American Dream, rests upon an understanding of equality and freedom that are deeply rooted in the infinite worth of the individual and a theocentric view of ultimate reality. Moreover, it is the vision of a multi-ethnic, multiracial, and interreligious civil society in which equality and freedom of the individual form the bedrock of national interests and policy. For Thurman, the Declaration of Independence, the Constitution, and the Emancipation Proclamation are the pivotal documents of the American civic and moral experience. These civil documents hold out the hope of individual freedom and equality under God and remind Americans of their role as stewards of the democratic ideal. He also refers to Lincoln's Gettysburg Address as a mandate for the rejuvenation of a "new nation" entrusted with the moral responsibility of realizing the democratic ideal in the world with other nations. With the potential for nuclear devastation wrought by the creation of the atomic bomb and, presumably, the rapid development of nuclear technology in the 1970s, Thurman also strikes a foreboding note that it may be too late to realize the American Dream.[4]

---

3. "Neighborliness," Thurman held, is "the immediate awareness of the pushing out of the barriers of self, the moment we flow together into one, when I am not male or female, yellow or green or black or white or brown, educated or illiterate, rich or poor, sick or well, righteous or unrighteous—but a naked human spirit that spills into other human spirits as they spill into me"; HT, "The Commitment" (March 1949), in *PHWT*, 3: 309. Peter Eisenstadt writes, "Thurman, like all African Americans, was an expert in navigating the geographic complexities and spatial consequences of racial separation"; Peter Eisenstadt, "Neighborliness Is Nonspatial": Howard Thurman and the Search for Integration and Common Ground," *Journal of Urban History* 46, no. 6 (2017): 1206–21; http://journals.sagepub.com/doi/10.1177/0096144217703543.

4. As early as 1951, Thurman used the metaphor of "school is out" as a statement of the urgency to begin to repair the damage to the democratic experiment wrought by

Now, school is out. School is out, and it's been out for some time. And the soul of America that is seeking to realize itself in the life of America is revealed by the degree to which the enforced experience of neighborhoods, which represents our 200 years, can be a living, practicing part of neighborliness, which is the fulfillment of the dream.

L adies and gentlemen, I want to begin tonight by reading two things: First, the Gettysburg Address. Second, "It's a Strange Freedom," from *The Inward Journey.*[5]

It is a strange freedom to be adrift in the world of men without a sense of anchor anywhere. Always there is the need of mooring, the need for the firm grip on something that is rooted and will not give. The urge to be accountable to someone, to know that beyond the individual himself there is an answer that must be given, cannot be denied. The deed a man performs must be weighed in a balance held by another's hand. The very spirit of a man tends to panic from the desolation of going nameless up and down the streets of other minds where no salutation greets and no friendly recognition makes secure. It is a strange freedom to be adrift in the world of men.

Always a way must be found for bringing into one's solitary place the settled look from another's face, for getting the quiet sanction of another's grace to undergird the meaning of the self. To be ignored, to be passed over as of no account and of no meaning, is to be made into a faceless thing, not a man. It is better to be the complete victim of an anger unrestrained and a wrath which knows no bounds, to be torn asunder without mercy or battered to a pulp by angry violence, than to be passed over as if one were not. Here at least one is dealt with, encountered, vanquished, or over-

---

the arrogance of imperialism and military might. See "A Faith to Live By: Democracy and the Individual I," printed in this volume.

5. HT, "A Strange Freedom," in *The Inward Journey* (Richmond, IN: Friends United Press, 1980), 37–38.

whelmed—but not ignored. It is a strange freedom to go nameless up and down the streets of other minds where no salutation greets and no sign is given to mark the place one calls one's own.

The name marks the claim a man stakes against the world; it is the private banner under which he moves which is his right whatever else betides. The name is a man's water mark above which the tides can never rise. It is the thing he holds that keeps him in the way when every light has failed and every marker has been destroyed. It is the rallying point around which a man gathers all that he means by himself. It is his announcement of life that he is present and accounted for in all his parts. To be made anonymous and to give to it the acquiescence of the heart is to live without life, and for such a one, even death is not dying.

I begin my thinking with you tonight from a background and out of the insight of a man who is earnestly engaged in an effort, an exercise, a commitment to be a religious man. I do not deal with the subject as one in a political field, but as one in the world of religion. I begin then my thinking about the subject from within the framework of certain basic religious affirmations. It is these that I want to state as directly and simply as possible.

It is my affirmation, my faith, that God is the Creator of Life. And not merely Life, but the Creator of the living substance out of which all particular manifestations of life emerge in the first place. Further, I believe that God is the Creator of existence, that God bottoms existence. So that from within the framework of my thought the totality of life on this planet—with all of its limitations, its fresh starts, its false starts, its rising and its falling—all of this is a lung through which the Creator of Life is bringing his breath into particular beings and manifestations.[6]

---

6. In Thurman's *The Search for Common Ground: An Inquiry into the Basis of Man's Experience of Community* (New York: Harper & Row, 1971), his most philosophical exposition of the nature of community, he addresses this central theme in a similar way, "The degree to which the potential in any expression of life is actualized marks the extent to which an expression of life experiences wholeness, integration, community. The clue to community can be found in the inner creative activity of living substances" (4). In an earlier lecture entitled "Community and the Will of God," Thurman says: "Community, or the functional and creative wholeness,

Therefore, I feel that Life is alive. Now this concept is so simple that perhaps the mind has some difficulty in reducing it to a manageable unit as an object of thought. But to me it is the aliveness of Life that provides the creative, churning continuum out of which all existences arise in the first place. The mind is so overwhelmed by the massive attack of all of these particular representations of vitality that the simplest fact of all is overlooked, that Life itself is alive, is a living, breathing, pulsing, universal, total experience. When I think of America, when I think of the American "dream," if dream is the right word, I do not think of it outside of a structure of the kind that I have stated.

I begin with the simple fact that America, however we may define it for ourselves, is an expression of one creative process coming into being more and more as its inner mystery, which is inherent in Life, begins to unfold as process, as laws, as constitutions. Therefore, my first notion for your consideration, with all of this as a background, is that the soul of America is being sought as a part of its unfolding with the soul of America as a part of the given. It is not an accident to me that at a particular time in the history of our world, there came to this continent, in a most extraordinary way, groups of people with different backgrounds, with different interests, with different cultural idioms to land themselves among a people who were as different in terms of ethos, in terms of dreams, hopes, aspirations as one could possibly imagine; and that without any apparent intentions of initially establishing a new order, a new way of living, a new series of expressions of the common life, there emerged, as a result of that experience, something that was referred to in Lincoln's famous Gettysburg address as "a new nation," conceived as a new idea for a nation.[7]

We have developed a society in which the experience of community springing out of a common commitment which grew out of a common crisis is the binding factor. At first, apparently, there was no intention to

---

is a manifest tendency in life itself, that the intent of the Creator of Life gives to all forms of life the communal potential, that the degree to which the potential becomes actualized, community results"; Mendenhall Lectures, DePauw University (February 1961), HTC. He applies this reasoning to the United States of America as a "living entity."

7. The opening sentence of Lincoln's "Gettysburg Address" is "Four score and seven years ago our fathers brought forth on this continent, a new nation, conceived in Liberty, and dedicated to the proposition that all men are created equal."

establish any kind of new world, any kind of new order, so that from my point of view it seems to me that the fact that America became America, a new people, a new order, a new political arrangement, was a part of the revelation of the Creator working itself out in the time-space relationships between men in a strange and awkward world. But the thing that appeals to me most directly is that these people who came from Europe and from other parts of the world were knit together by political ideas and ideals which were not created by them, but which represented a creative synthesis which revealed a projection of their own hopes and fears, dreams and aspirations. It found formal statement in a Declaration of Independence, in a Bill of Rights, in a Constitution, in a form of government unique in many ways. As circumstantial as that may be, there is something still more circumstantial, which, from my point of view, is miraculous. It took place in North America—a land isolated from the stable civilized communal arrangements in Europe, and protected by two oceans, in a climate almost ideal. Even Californians must share with the rest of the country the glory of this idyllic natural circumstance.

Now get the picture. Here was a cross section of people with a medley of cultural backgrounds and orientations, but all within a broad European pattern, landing in the midst of what seems to have been an indigenous people, isolated by two oceans, in a climate in which all of the basic creature needs and demands of life could be fulfilled by minimal effort. This cross section of people was inspired by a political idea and a political theory which could only be developed within a sufficient time interval to test whether or not they, the people of the colonies, could accommodate themselves not only to each other, but also to the Indians whom they found here. It was as if the Creator of Life and existence was anticipating another moment in time far removed from this moment in history of which I speak.

They were a diverse people in a fertile land, a benevolent and beneficent land, brooded over by a political theory rooted in a certain way of thinking about the nature of life and the nature of existence—brooding over it as the spirit of the hives broods over the places where the bees make honey. (Once the spirit of the hive is no longer brooding, the bee cannot make honey; he's just another insect.) This was a political theory inspired by a fundamental way of thinking about the nature of life and the nature of man, with a time interval of sufficient duration to provide the opportunity, not the necessity, mark my word, but the opportunity, for growth in relatedness, for primary face-to-face discovery of the secret of a life far removed from one's own background and culture. In other words, the opportunity to experience community, an inner sense of relatedness defined by the external boundaries within which life is being lived. It was as if the Creator of existence wanted to discover whether or not a certain ideal could be realized in time and space, in anticipation of a time when time and space would be reduced to zero; when the whole planet would be as one little neighborhood in one little town.

This meant that somewhere on the planet there would be a primary unit of human beings being tutored in the graces of communal relatedness, crossing lines of race, of color, or creed, or background, of enforced or restricted neighborhoods. Nowhere else on the planet was this taking place. Nowhere else. And all of this would occur before the creative mind of modern man was to grapple with the stubborn and unyielding and recalcitrant stuff of nature, until at last by his intensive and sophisticated science, grudgingly, the secrets of nature would be revealed and the mind would seize upon the secrets and use them in pursuit of private ends. Suppose that man had developed the secret of the atom, and all of the other devices by which we have reduced time and space to zero, before there had been this colossal experience, this exposure to neighborliness? We live in panic now lest some man whose digestion goes awry will, in a moment of pain or panic, reach out and touch the wrong button. But the anxiety and fear that dog the footsteps of modern man is not to be compared with what would have happened if the whole process had been reversed—if nowhere on this planet there had been the opportunity to experience growth in community day by day, hard year by hard year, in the midst of all kinds of struggle. But the Creator of existence, I think, was trying to see if it were possible for him to realize himself, to come to himself, not in an individual expression of his creation, but in *the collective* sense; not by mindless instinct-bound creatures, but by those created in his own image.

So he said, "I wonder if I dare do this?" He tested it in all ways his great creativity could figure out: "I'll set up somewhere a school and I'll call that school, America." (Now don't be upset by what seems to be a doctrine of manifest destiny.[8] Don't be bothered by that.) "But I'll set up a school somewhere and I'll time it well, so that it will pre-date some other secrets that I'm going to give to my children, the secret of my energy, so that there will be a backlog of accumulated social and political experience, ethical, moral, religious experience if you please, upon which my children may draw totally and I'll make some dry runs while I'm doing this."

Now, school is out. School is out, and it's been out for some time. And the soul of America that is seeking to realize itself in the life of America is revealed by the degree to which the enforced experience of neighborhoods, which represents our two hundred years, can be a living, practicing part of neighborliness, which is the fulfillment of the dream.

We have worked at this. I think the two principles that have been guideposts for this as they emerged in the great Declaration, which is a sort of mandate, have to do with definitions—pragmatic definitions, practical definitions, empirical definitions—of equality and freedom.

One comment about the first. When I think about the meaning of equality against this background, I think of many kinds of definitions. Some, the result of the fact that I'm a child of these times: Equality of opportunity. Equality of privilege. Equality of gifts. But in every one of these there is the germ of a cult that seeks to nullify this equality. This is the Cult of Inequality.[9]

So that I am stripped to what seems to me to be the literal essence of my own pulse beat in which the sense of equality is grounded—that is the sense of my own self, my own self. My own self as distinguished from your self. My own self, of infinite worth and significance. This may be, perhaps, the only authentic equality that there is. I've been worrying over all of this for a long time. *The equality of infinite worth.* That is my truest experience of myself. That is not a derivative from any judgment external to myself; that is not located in any extension of myself, not located

8. "Manifest destiny," a term coined in the 1840s and officially invoked throughout the nineteenth century, alleged the inevitable territorial expansion of the United States to the Pacific Coast. The term was also invoked to justify U.S. takeovers of Hawaii and of Spanish colonies in the Atlantic and Pacific after the Spanish-American War.

9. Thurman made a similar argument in "The Fascist Masquerade" (1946), repr. in *PHWT,* 3: 145–62.

in any extenuating circumstances with regard to myself, not related to any definition that does not arise out of that, out of which, at last, the true grounds of my own self-respect arise. This definition of equality is implicit then in that aspect of the soul of America that is still in the process of realizing itself, in institutions, in communal relations, in social arrangements, and in the security of its laws.

In the winter of the middle thirties my wife and I traveled some 16,000 miles in India, Burma, and Ceylon visiting colleges and universities.[10] It was a difficult time because whenever we came down to tight, analytical discussions with Indian students, whether they were Hindu, Buddhists, or Christians, they always said to us, "We are so much better off than you are." They were still under British rule.[11] "We are so much better off than you are because" ... and then go on to give a variety of reasons. Then I would say that one important difference between their society and ours was that brooding over all of the inequities in our society is a Supreme Court. And therefore, the final interpretations of the genius of the democratic dogma was given into the hands of men whose job it was to monitor the life of the nation by the profoundest interpretations of the meaning of the Constitution and the Bill of Rights. This the students did not have. There was always the possibility for me, which for the Indians simply wasn't true, that there was at work in the structure of American society that which is always involved in condemning that which violates the spirit and the genius of the democratic dogma itself.

The second summary statement bearing on all of this has to do with freedom. When I think about freedom it is always from the point of view of the true distinction between freedom and liberty. As I interpret the American story, liberty has to do primarily with elements of the social contract. It can be given; it can be taken away. It can be wiped out. It is related to external but very important agreements within the structure of the society itself. Therefore, it can be altered by law, improved, destroyed, prostituted, or glorified. But that was not what was meant by freedom originally. Freedom, as defined in the slow development of the language of the Constitution, had to be redefined many times. What was finally

---

10. For a full accounting of the Pilgrimage of Friendship, see *PHWT*, vol. 1.

11. The period of direct British rule over the Indian subcontinent extended from 1858 until the independence of India and Pakistan in 1947.

being said was that freedom is a quality of being. It cannot be given and it cannot be taken away. Liberty can be taken away. But freedom! Freedom is the process by which, standing in my place where I am, I can so act in that place as to influence, order, alter, or change the future—that time is not frozen, that life is not so fixed that it cannot respond to my own will, my own inner *processes*. Standing in my place I can so order my life and varied dimensions of my environment as to influence, and often determine and shape, the future.

But it is more than this. It is the private, intimate, primary exercise of a profound and unique sense of alternatives. Now this is very important. Freedom, as it was thought of in that far-off time, and as it has been working itself out for at least two hundred years—freedom is the sense of option. Mark you, I do not say that freedom is the exercise of option. That may not be possible. But freedom is the sense of option, the sense of alternatives which only I can affect. And this is the thing that threatens all dictatorships, all tyrants, because there is not any way which the external forces in the environment can reach inside and cause the individual human spirit to relax and give up its sense of option.

Let me illustrate. When I was a boy, living in Florida, I went with my sister one summer day out into the woods near our house to pick huckleberries. I was younger than she. I was always trying to grow up, and she was always trying to cut off my growth. As we walked along the country road I noticed a baby snake about the length of my foot. I knew how she felt about old snakes, young snakes, baby snakes, any kind of snake. I saw it before she did, and I said to myself, "Now is my chance." And so I said, "Henrietta, look at this." And she reacted. And then I said, "Oh, I'm not afraid of it. To show you I'll stand on it." So I put one of my feet on top of this little creature and the weight of my body made it impossible for him to move. Then I felt a series of simple, quiet, rhythmic spasms under my foot. The snake couldn't move, but he could do this wiggle. He kept alive the sense of option. Even though he couldn't opt the options. Now this is what I mean: that freedom is a sense of option, and wherever this dies, wherever elements in the environment are internalized by people so as to paralyze this sense, then all the lights go out and the soul of the people begins to rot.

Now this carries with it very definite responsibilities, and these responsibilities are the safeguard against the degradation of the democratic dogma. One is a sense of responsibility for one's own actions. [Without this],[12] something is cut off. The oxygen is taken out of the air and the person dies, perishes. That is why I think the myth of George Washington and the cherry tree has remained in our culture. "I did it with my little hatchet. I did it!"

There is the second aspect of freedom that belongs in any discussion about it, and that is that freedom is my own responsibility for my own reactions *to* the events, the forces, the influences that impinge upon my life, that are not responsive to my will, however good that will may be— impersonal forces that don't even know that as an individual I am here. But I must deal with them at the point at which they touch my life. And I can say, you see, that it is not my fault that forces, alien to my mind and spirit, created this situation that results in my predicament. True this may be, but I'm not relieved if I would be free. I must take the responsibility for how, mark my word, *how* I react to the forces that impinge upon my life, forces that are not responsive to my will, my desire, my ambition, my dream, my hope—forces that don't know that I'm here. But I know I'm here. And I decide whether I will say *yes* or *no,* and make it hold. This indeed is the free man, and this is anticipated in the genius of the dogma of freedom as a manifestation of the soul of America, born in what to me is one of the greatest of the great experiments in human relations.

Heir of the kingdom 'neath the skies
Often he falls yet falls to rise
Stumbling, bleeding, beaten back
Holding still to the upper track
Playing his part in Creation's plan
God-like in image, this is Man.
This is Man.[13]

---

12. Editors' insertion.

13. One of Thurman's favorite poems. It appears, attributed to "an unidentified writer," in Robert Scott and William C. Stiles, eds., *Cyclopedia of Illustrations for Public Speakers* (New York: Funk & Wagnalls, 1911), 446. Thurman used the poem to close the final sermon he ever preached, in October 1980; see *PHWT,* 5: 317.

Appendix I

Meditation on the Rosenbergs

June 21, 1953
Fellowship Church

Thurman only rarely commented directly on political events in his Sunday sermons.[1] On June 21, 1953, he devoted the bulk of his sermon at Fellowship Church to the twentieth-century American mystic Jane Steger.[2] The opening meditation was on an entirely different subject. Two days earlier, Julius and Ethel Rosenberg had been executed at Sing Sing Prison in New York State for espionage.[3] Since their arrest, three years earlier, on charges of passing information to the Soviet Union about the United States nuclear weapons program, the case had become one of the greatest causes célèbres of the early Cold War. The Rosenbergs, members of the Communist Party, always denied the espionage accusations. Many on the non-communist left, like Thurman and presumably most members of Fellowship Church, either believed them innocent or had doubts about their guilt, and certainly felt that their sentences were far too harsh. They were the only civilians executed for espionage in American history.[4]

---

1. For other exceptions, see Hjalmar Petersen, "A Brief Historical Sketch and Visit with President Roosevelt," copy in the Howard Thurman Papers (an account of a visit to Fellowship Church and Thurman's comments on the Sunday after the death of President Franklin D. Roosevelt); "Mahatma Gandhi," in *PHWT*, 3: 248–53, delivered on February 1, 1949, two days after Gandhi's assassination.

2. See "Jane Steger," in HT, *The Way of the Mystics*, ed. Peter Eisenstadt and Walter E. Fluker (Maryknoll, NY: Orbis Books, 2021), 72–81.

3. Julius (1918–1953) and Ethel (1915–1953) Rosenberg were native and lifelong residents of New York City, active in the Communist Party from their teenage years.

4. Since the fall of the Soviet Union, documents have been released that demonstrate conclusively that Julius Rosenberg was part of a Soviet espionage ring, though Ethel's connection to the espionage ring was, if it existed, far more tenuous.

This is among the most despairing and darkly pessimistic of all of Thur-man's political statements, comparable only to some of his comments after the assassination of Martin Luther King Jr.[5] Although Thurman was never a communist, and took pains to prevent members of the Communist Party from gaining influence in the church, he was equally upset by anti-communist hysteria in early 1950s America.[6] (Like many others with a history of involvement with liberal and progressive causes, Thurman was a target of FBI surveillance from the early 1940s through the late 1960s.)[7] For Thurman, the vindictive spirit that demanded the death of the Rosenbergs epitomized the "grossness and callousness and insensitiveness and brutality . . . that petrifies the spirit," which he found to be so rampant and repulsive in the United States in 1953.

Meditation[8]

There is great confusion and despair, disorder, because we have been part of something which makes naked the spirit and the mind of man. We have visited death on two human beings, whose deed, by the judgment of the court, merited death. And even where there are those whose minds are sure that the logic of the law has fulfilled itself, that justice has been done, a position before the world declared and defined, even there lurking

---

Most historians of the episode believe that Ethel was sentenced to death to put pressure on Julius to confess, but neither ever admitted any role in Soviet espionage activities. Other document releases in recent years have also revealed the range of prosecutorial misconduct in the trial and sentencing of the Rosenbergs; see Walter Schneir, *Final Verdict: What Really Happened in the Rosenberg Case* (Brooklyn, NY: Melville House, 2010).

5. See "Martin Luther King, Jr.: Litany and Words in Memoriam," delivered at Fellowship Church, April 7, 1968, in *PHWT*, 5: 176–88.

6. For a review of Thurman's complex attitudes toward communism, see Peter Eisenstadt, "Howard Thurman, Martin Luther King, Jr., the Cold War, the Civil Rights Movement, and Postwar Liberal Black Protestantism," in Paul Mojzes, ed., *North American Churches and the Cold War* (Grand Rapids, MI: William B. Eerdmans, 2018), 194–205.

7. See "Howard Thurman's FBI Files, 1942–1968," printed in the current volume.

8. Unnamed Meditation, dated "July 21, 1953," but delivered on Sunday, June 21, 1953.

within the shadows of the mind and spirit, there is the great misgiving, the foreboding shadow of a tremendous doubt.

What shall we say to God today, in our own land, in our own country—what can we say to him? Can we say to him that we were afraid and our fears mounted and mounted until at last, in our desperation, we acted without compassion and with vengeance? Can he understand this in us? Can we say to him that because of the imperfections of the world and the sickness that lays waste the hearts of nations and peoples, that we are moving in a great delirium and that not altogether are we responsible for what we do? Can he understand that? When we say it to him?

Can we say to him that we are guilty of so much grossness and callousness and insensitiveness and brutality that our hearts have become weary in so much anguish and hardened themselves in quiet defense against disintegration? Can he understand what it means in all the ways that petrify the spirit? And clogs all the inlets? From that which renews and restores the hearts of man? What can we say to God today as we sit in the shadows nursing our fears and clutching the hands of two orphaned children?[9] What can we say to God? What *can* we say?

---

9. Michael (b. 1943) and Robert (b. 1947) Meeropol, who kept the names of the family that adopted them after the execution of their parents.

Appendix II

Howard Thurman's FBI Files, 1942–1968

The Federal Bureau of Investigation (FBI), under its longtime director, J. Edgar Hoover,[1] created a vast index of persons deemed to be potentially dangerous to national security. Many of these individuals were included in the index because of their real or supposed connection to the communist movement. Howard Thurman was one of them. He was included in the FBI index from 1942 on, though the first of three memoranda on his status was written only in 1955, after an informant denounced Thurman for spreading "Communistic" ideas. This was an absurd accusation. Although Thurman's politics were left of center, and he was sympathetic to some of the causes of the Communist Party, he was never a party member, nor was he ever particularly close to it or its affiliated organizations.[2] The files also noted that he was a member of the advisory board of CORE and a member of the ACLU, neither of which were in any way associated with the Communist Party. His financial support for the other organizations mentioned in the files is certainly possible though unproven.

In 1966 Thurman served as a public member of the selection board of the U.S. Foreign Service in an effort to increase the number of Black foreign service officers.[3] Presumably this required a security clearance, but by the time the FBI had finished its background check, Thurman had completed

---

1. J. Edgar Hoover (1895–1972) was director of the FBI from 1924 to 1972. He systematically abused the civil liberties of millions of Americans and showed a special animus toward African American activists.

2. For Thurman and communism, see Eisenstadt, *Against the Hounds of Hell*, 168–69, 256–60. See also Peter Eisenstadt, "Howard Thurman, Martin Luther King, Jr., the Cold War, the Civil Rights Movement, and Postwar Liberal Black Protestantism," in Paul Mojzes, ed., *North American Churches and the Cold War* (Grand Rapids, MI: William B. Eerdmans, 2018), 194–205.

3. See *PHWT*, 5, 162–64.

his time on the selection board. J. Edgar Hoover himself wrote a memo-
randum about Thurman, concluding that further investigation of Thur-
man was moot. Nonetheless, a third memorandum, written the following
year, summarizes the information about Thurman known to the FBI.
Unlike many others, Thurman apparently did not suffer any personal or
professional repercussions from his surveillance by the FBI. The editors have
printed the three memoranda in the order in which they appear in Thur-
man's file, which is not chronological. The raw files have been edited for space
considerations and to eliminate bureaucratic redundancies.

Subject: Thurman, Howard Washington
File Number: 100–417823
Office Memorandum: United States Government
Date: 3/29/55
To: Director, FBI
From: SAC[4] Cincinnati (100-5)
Subject: Reverend Howard Thurman, Security Matter

On 3/18/55 REDACTED telephonically advised SA of this office,
that he had information concerning an individual that he felt should be
brought to the attention of the FBI.

REDACTED advised that he recently attended services in Cincinnati, Ohio, and noted that Reverend HOWARD THURMAN, D.D.,
Dean of Daniel L. Marsh Chapel, Boston, Massachusetts, was to be the
speaker during the Lenten ceremonies at Christ Church from March 28,
1955 to April 1, 1955.

REDACTED advised that he felt Reverend THURMAN was one
who should be of interest to this organization. He stated that while he
was attending the baccalaureate services at Western College for Women
at Oxford, Ohio, Reverend THURMAN was the principal speaker.[5] He
stated that Reverend THURMAN was "radical" and advocated "Com-

---

4. Special Agent in Charge.
5. Thurman delivered the commencement address at the Western College for
Women, in Oxford, OH, on May 23, 1954. This was four days after the U.S. Supreme
Court issued its ruling in Brown v. Board of Education. Whether Thurman spoke

munism." He stated that he could not recall offhand the exact wording of Reverend THURMAN's talk, but it was such that only a person with a clear understanding of his topic would realize the Communistic implications.

REDACTED stated of his previous experience with Reverend THURMAN and felt that this matter should be brought to the attention of the FBI in the event Reverend THURMAN was traveling around the country speaking in behalf of Communism.

An investigation of the Cincinnati indices disclosed that Reverend HOWARD THURMAN was listed as a member of the Advisory Committee of the Committee of Racial Equality which maintains its principal office in New York City.[6]

JHZ:alc

This matter is being brought to the attention of the Bureau, and the Boston Office is being requested to furnish any information of Communistic activities on the part of Reverend THURMAN that might be contained in their files. No further action is being taken by the Cincinnati Division unless advised by the Bureau.

October 18, 1968
Summary
HOWARD THURMAN, DD
Born: November 18, 1900
Daytona Beach, Florida

No investigation has been conducted relative to the subject of your name check request. A review of the files of this Bureau reveals the following information.

In 1948, a source, who had furnished reliable information in the past, made available a list of names maintained by the Joint Anti-Fascist Refugee Committee and its subsidiary group, the Spanish Refugee Appeal,

---

about the decision in his address is not known, but he did comment in a similar address a week later; see Eisenstadt, *Against the Hounds of Hell*, 287.

6. Thurman had been an informal advisor to CORE (Congress of Racial Equality) from its formation in 1942, and was a member of its advisory board from 1945 to 1966; see *PHWT*, 2: 323–24; 3: 133–34; 5: 140–44.

San Francisco, California. Included on this list was one Howard Thurman (Rev. Dr.), 2660 California Street, San Francisco.[7]

Another source, who had furnished reliable information in the past, advised in 1948 that the above list of names was current as of March 17, 1948 . . . The Joint Anti-Fascist Refugee Committee has been cited by the Attorney General of the United States pursuant to Executive Order 10450.[8]

In 1942, another source, who had furnished reliable information in the past, made available material pertaining to the Citizens to Free Earl Browder.[9] Among this data was a sample resolution containing the name of 163 prominent clergymen who had petitioned for the release of Earl Browder. One Howard Thurman, Baptist, Washington, D.C., was listed thereon.

The Citizens Committee to Free Earl Browder has been cited by the Attorney General of the United States pursuant to Executive Order 10450.

In October 1951 REDACTED made available various documents purporting to be part of the Institute of Pacific Relations[10] files. Included was an updated list of Washington, D.C., members. The name of one

---

7. The Joint Anti-Fascist Refugee Committee (JAFRC) was created in 1941 as a successor to several earlier efforts by veterans of the Abraham Lincoln Brigade, the American fighting force recruited by the Communist International to fight on the side of the Spanish Republicans. The organization had a large number of non-communist supporters, among them Albert Einstein, Thomas Mann, and Langston Hughes. After harassment from the House Committee on Un-American Activities and the Departments of the Treasury and Justice, the organization disbanded in 1955.

8. Executive Order 10450 was issued in April 1953. It barred "security risks" from federal employment, a group that included gays and lesbians, and those with contacts with a large list of organizations the Justice Department deemed subversive. Although its scope had been considerably narrowed, Executive Order 10450 was not fully repealed until January 2017, in one of the last acts of the Obama administration.

9. The Citizens Committee to Free Earl Browder was in existence from 1941 to 1942. Earl Browder (1891–1973) was general secretary of the Communist Party, USA, from 1930 to 1945. He served a sentence in a federal penitentiary from 1941 to 1942 for a passport violation. The committee, like many organized by the Communist Party during the Popular Front era, sought the support of many non-communists.

10. The Institute of Pacific Relations, organized in 1925 to study the politics of the Pacific region, came under intense attack during World War II and the Cold War for its alleged communist sympathies. It disbanded in 1960.

Dean Howard Thurman, Rankin Memorial Chapel, Howard University, appeared on the list.

The guide to Subversive Organizations and Publications, revised and published December 1, 1961, prepared and released by the Committee on Un-American Activities, United States House of Representatives, page 87, cites the Institute of Pacific Relations as a communist front . . .

The San Francisco Office by report dated May 26, 1956, captioned [REDACTED] IS-CH San Francisco file 105-1049 refers on page 2 to an article appearing in the January 15 issue of "Palo Alto Times" entitled "News of the Communities," which reported that Dr. Howard Thurman was a member of the American Civil Liberties Union.[11]

Date: February 6, 1967
To: Director, Bureau of Personnel Investigations, Civil Service Commission
From: John Edgar Hoover, Director
Subject: HOWARD WASHINGTON THURMAN
          Department of State
          SECURITY OF GOVERNMENT EMPLOYEES
          CSS #NY.67.052213

Reference is made to information previously furnished to the Civil Service Commission that an appropriate investigation has been initiated by this Bureau under the provisions of Executive Order 10450.

Information has now been received from a review of Thurman's Official Personnel Folder on February 2, 1967, that he served as a Consultant (Public Member of 20th Selection Board for Foreign Service Officers), Office of Performance Evaluation from September 10, 1966, until December 8, 1966, when his temporary excepted appointment was terminated because of completion of his assignment.

In view of the above, no further investigation will be conducted by the Bureau regarding captioned matter.

---

11. The American Civil Liberties Union, since its founding in 1920, has been a prominent liberal organization defending the legal rights of individuals and organizations against government interference and repression.

INDEX OF NAMES

Nancy, Jean-Luc, xxin36
Neal, Anthony Sean, 103n4
Nebuchadnezzar (Neo-Babylonian king), 20
Niebuhr, Reinhold, 75, 75n3

Paul (New Testament apostle), 12, 13, 13n8, 16
Petersen, Hjalmar, 125n1
Plato, 34n5, 86, 87n7, 87n8
Popper, Karl, 87n7

Rancière, Jacques, xxin36
Robert, J. Deotis, 102, 103n3
Roosevelt, Franklin D., 78, 78–79n7, 83n1, 125n1
Rosenberg, Ethel, xiv, 125, 125n3, 125–26n4, 126
Rosenberg, Julius, xiv, 125, 125n3, 125–26n4, 126
Royce, Josiah, 10, 10n4, 11, 11n4, 11n5, 15, 18, 19

Saillant, John, xxivn45
Santayana, George, 11n4
Schneir, Walter, 126n4
Schreiner, Olive, 44, 44n3, 107n7

Schweitzer, Albert, 50n12
Scott, Charles E., xxin36
Slate, Nico, xixn33
Smith, Luther E., xxn34, xxii, xxiin39, 103n4
Sophocles, 86n5
Steger, Jane, 125, 125n2
Stendahl, Krister, 13n8
Story, William Wetmore, 91n11

Thurman, Sue Bailey, xxix, xxixn62
Tracy, Hannah R., 44n3
Tumber, Cathy, xxin38, 114n1

Van Dyke, Henry, 20, 21, 21n5

Walker, Corey D. B., 104n4
Washington, George, 34, 35n8, 124
Weil, Simone, 107n8
Weinberg, Rabbi Dudley, 99n9
Welles, Sumner, 83n1
Wells, H. G., 99n8
Whittier, John Greenleaf, 55n3
Wiggins, William H., Jr. 93n1
Wilson, Woodrow, 21n5
Woodward, C. Vann, 110n13

Made in the USA
Coppell, TX
10 October 2024

38453690R00094